16/11

£3—

ga

The Public Face of the Gospel

J. L. Houlden

The Public Face of the Gospel

New Testament Ideas of the Church

SCM PRESS LTD

Copyright © J. L. Houlden 1997

0 334 02666 0

First published 1997
by SCM Press Ltd
9–17 St Albans Place, London N1 0NX

Typeset by Regent Typesetting, London
and printed in Great Britain by
Biddles Ltd, Guildford and King's Lynn

Contents

Preface

This book gives an account of the institutional mode of early Christianity and the ideas in which it was expressed. That mode has been crucial and infinitely problematic in subsequent history in relation to so many aspects of human life: politics, warfare, art, literature, quite apart from the obviously religious sphere with which these have been inextricably interwoven. From some points of view, the institution has been more influential than the more purely conceptual aspects of the Christian religion which are generally deemed more central to its being – and we have learnt the futility of drawing hard and fast lines between them. At the same time, the church itself has from the start been the subject of beliefs or patterns of ideas. There was never a time when it was not theorized about. It has not simply functioned as a sphere of human activity, but has also been reflected on, sometimes in its own right, more often, particularly in the early period, in close con-nection with beliefs about God and his purposes, about Christ and salvation. The ways of thinking about the church, in the context of Christian faith as a whole, are the subject of this book.

People may approach these matters with an antiquarian interest, but more often they do so with at least half an eye on modern situations relating to the Christian community. That element of duality is not absent here, and comes to the fore in the final chapter. If you are in a tradition, after all, you must know it, face it as clearsightedly as you can, and understand yourself the better for the experience, even if you then choose to put aside many aspects of it or to re-cast them for new use. This book works towards the question: how, in the light of these matters of history, may we weigh up our own situation? To keep the discussion moving, continuous prose is preferred to excessive documentation.

Not for the first time, I owe thanks to John Bowden and the staff at SCM Press for encouraging and receiving this book, and to students at King's College, London, who, if they read it, may recognize its antecedents.

This little book is offered in gratitude to the church of St John the Evangelist, Goose Green, in South London, where it has been my privilege to serve as a priest for almost twenty years and where I have learnt much about the church's true glory.

Leslie Houlden
June 1996

Introduction

Scope and perspective

It is customary to think of a religion as a system of beliefs. So we read that 'Christianity teaches . . .' or 'Christians believe . . .' The former statement is verifiable in a formal way by reference to official statements of belief – creeds and the like. But it does not take much historical investigation to recognize that behind the official forms of words lie controversy and compromise, both in their origin, often many centuries ago, and in their use and interpretation over the years. The latter form of words can even more easily seem hollow. You do not have to be a very persistent sociologist, going round with your clip-board, to discover that Christians are very diverse indeed in the beliefs they hold and the relation of those beliefs to what 'Christianity teaches'. What is more, this is found to be the case at all levels of sophistication and within (not just between) all but the most tight-knit Christian groups – and even they have a strong tendency to disintegrate for this very reason. Whatever holds Christians together in their various communities or traditions, large and small, it is only rarely a narrow and fixed uniformity of belief – despite the efforts and claims of their leaders and cohesion-mongers. It seems inadequate to think of a religion simply as an identifiable system of beliefs. Such a definition is too cerebral and bland to do justice to the human and historical complexities that make up the being of a religion.

To try again: a religion is a network of human relationships, usually extended over both time and space, centring on certain beliefs and attitudes, and focussed on certain institutions and practices, both cultic and moral. That seems more rounded, altogether more realistic. In practice, and probably for most of the adherents of a religion, the institutions and practices loom larger than the beliefs. For many Jews and Christians in the West in the last two hundred years, even with the large-scale decline in religious observance, the institutions and some of the practices have indeed survived the virtual abandonment of many of the beliefs; though some of the latter commonly survive, even with tenacity, in attenuated, shadowy or (from a formal point of view) debased form. And for the external observer, the institutions and practices are what catch the eye – the building, the priest, the ceremony; while the beliefs remain hazy, rudimentary or arcane. It is moreover the church and its institutions and practices that more readily arouse passions and leaps to the barricades when change is mooted, no doubt because they relate to matters of routines, of sight, sound and action, much more palpable than abstract beliefs, though commonly it is felt desirable to back these passions, rooted in the senses, with abstract ideas, which may, or may not, relate convincingly to the central tenets of the religion concerned. It is partly in this perspective that we should no doubt view the extraordinary concentration (as it often seems to outsiders) of Christian controversy in recent decades (as indeed in the past) on matters relating to ordination and church structure and church relations, closely affecting Christians (or, to be frank, more commonly the clergy) in their worship and common life.

Much of this has been true from the beginning of Christianity. Yet when attention is given to Christian origins, institutional matters are often treated as peripheral, consigned to the final chapters of the book; unless, that is, they must be attended to for validating or despatching positions taken in modern church discussions. Of course belief about Jesus was always central to the being of Christianity; but the strong physical reference of that belief – it related to a man, notably distinctive in ideas, activities and suffering – subdued any tendency in the Christian movement to shun practicalities or to treat them as mere necessities of life: it was from the start concerned with the relations, organization and observances of human groups and with how to think about them, not least because of its Jewish matrix where most of such matters were of the essence.

While, like any other movement, Christianity has always been in flux, subject to change and adjustment in ways and degrees which its adherents have often been deeply reluctant to recognize, it has always set great store by its institutional character and incorporated its organization and common life into its intellectual structure, often by harking back (however unrealistically) to its origins as described in the New Testament. Nowadays, with our developed sense (as we feel it to be) of the social actualities of the ancient world, we should be less confident than our predecessors in tracing lines of simple continuity between then and now, still less in trying to reproduce the past in the present; though there is a false asceticism in declining to acknowledge points of contact where they are to be seen – Christian identity depends after all on some kind of publicly recognizable social and institutional continuum as well as the persistence of certain tendencies of thought and spiritual vision, however diverse their expression.

These identifiable points of continuity, notably the existence, in all its multitudinous forms, of the church itself as a community of believers and adherents, the structures of leadership within it, and the rites whereby it is entered (baptism) and sustains its life (eucharist and prayer), have been present as far back as the eye can see. In all these areas, beliefs have generally been closely related to the central mark of Christian identity, allegiance to Jesus as God's decisive agent for human well-being or salvation. They have also stubbed against social realities, which have not always been equally congenial to central Christian beliefs and dispositions. Sometimes indeed those realities have moulded both institutions and beliefs into conformity with ideas and ways of life where compatibility was strained to the uttermost. It is indeed arguable that many Christian bodies now live in such a time, with their distinctive vision submerged by secular pressures.

In this book I seek to describe how the Christians of the first two generations both thought and acted in relation to the Christian community, thought and action constraining each other with variety and subtlety. Some of the evidence is indirect, fragmentary and hard to evaluate: the documents were not written for the direct illumination of future generations on these (or indeed any) matters. Occasionally, however, as in some of Paul's letters, there are moments of relative luminosity.

In attending to origins, we need not shut our minds to subsequent developments. Continuities are often tenuous or relate only to one or two threads in a complex skein and we should resist the impulse to discern them where they do not exist. Similarly, we need not forget the perplexities and challenges of the present. The New Testament is in no position to provide copy-book solutions: the days when it could be pressed convincingly into that role are well in the past. But it may give certain kinds of orientation or move us to adopt (and reject) certain priorities that now present themselves. Chiefly and simply, it will recall us to the gospel. At least it may jerk us out of some of the grooves of modern controversy and lead us to recognize how constant is the interweaving of belief and human practicalities. We see the futility in reckoning belief to be a matter of pure abstraction or interiority, separable from the rest of our being and immune to the full setting in which we live and hold faith. If liberation theology has taught us anything, it is that we should be aware of the effect of context on belief and welcome the propriety of that influence. The emphasis here will, however, mostly be on ideas, but without forgetting that ideas are held amid actualities.

The Christian phenomenon

The Christian movement, whose institutional embodiment is the subject of this book, was remarkable for the rapidity of its expansion from its original location in Palestine and for the effectiveness of its internal network of relationships and communication. These features, unparalleled in their intensity in any other movements of the period, are all the more remarkable in that there was no lack of obstacles to their achievement, not least serious internal divisions within the movement itself, even about its own proper identity. Above all, the early rift between the Christian community in Jerusalem, senior from every point of view, and Paul and his associates over the terms for the admission of gentile converts, might easily have shipwrecked the entire enterprise, at least as a unified activity. Perhaps that outcome was only averted by the disappearance of the Jerusalem church from the scene in the fall of the city in 70CE.

There was however a cost to the cutting of that tie; for the Jerusalem community, with its geographical and human links to Jesus and surely the venerable associations of its location (though admittedly little trace of such a feeling survives in our sources), provided, for all the difficulties, a visible centre for the Christian movement, one with a clear claim to authority, however much it might seem necessary to resist it; even though the numerical balance had probably shifted by the latter part of the century in favour of gentile membership. Now the movement was left with no such centre, no 'head', save the invisible Christ himself; though the Acts of the Apostles, with its twin foci of Jerusalem and Rome as the extremities of its story, ventures to suggest a new way of organizing the Christian mind geographically. It is an optimistic way that maximizes the past and looks to the future with confidence – that is on the assumption that Acts was written after Jerusalem's fall, an event which, in the light of its Spirit-inspired Christian strategy, it can ignore. The Pauline mission in particular had already operated, perforce, largely under its own steam, and distance had made close centralized direction no more feasible in the Christian than in the Jewish diaspora (despite forays of interference in Paul's mission from Jerusalem Christians); so that the new, post-70 CE situation was by no means as disastrous as might have been supposed and, from the point of view of the gentile churches, had distinct practical advantages, however genuine their reverence for the old Jewish scriptures which they had inherited. Nevertheless, the final decades of the first century witnessed a series of developments that may be construed not only as the institutionalizing changes normally associated with the second generation of new and charismatic movements but also as responses to a felt need for bearings and for sources of guidance. It is possible that even the writing of the gospels should be regarded in this light: the saving message must be embodied with pen and ink and durable papyrus. They record and evoke a Christian 'holy past', one that follows and is seen as in a sense continuous with that narrated in the Jewish scriptures. We can certainly ascribe the formalization of structures of leadership and worry over the credentials of those who occupy such positions (as for example in I Clement and I Timothy), at least partly, to such a need. It was also met by the re-working of history that we find in the Acts of the Apostles. There, the feuds of the past are over-painted with eirenic gloss, the trauma of near-break-up between Paul and Jerusalem (see Gal. 2.11ff.) dissolved in a healing balm of unity (Acts 15). The collecting of Paul's letters, so that they were gradually transformed from occasional communications into perpetual authorities, is surely part of the same process of grounding the movement more comfortably in its altered circumstances.

The same period saw the gradual establishment of Christianity as an entity distinct by all reasonable tests from Judaism. It might, in certain moods and in certain respects, assert its claim to be the 'fulfilment' of Judaism (whatever that usefully blurred word might be taken to mean) or even the 'true' Judaism – and the retention by the mainstream churches of the old scriptures testifies most clearly to that claim – but the separation, no doubt gradual and piecemeal and brought about by situations susceptible for some time of different interpretations in this regard, was virtually complete by the end of the first century. How far the factors that led to this separation were social in character and how far they were theological is open to discussion; but both the open admission policy for gentiles adopted by Paul and the heightening of Christian claims for Jesus, soon the object of worship, played major parts in forcing the issue.

But none of these transitions was as profound, as impressive or as perplexing as that which pre-dated them in the history of the Christian movement: that from the largely peripatetic work of Jesus to the settled life of Christian groups. The former was predominantly rural, the latter overwhelmingly urban; the former Palestinian, chiefly Aramaic-speaking, the latter (Jerusalem and perhaps a few other communities apart) Graeco-Roman and Greek-speaking; the former fairly characterized as 'a reform movement in Judaism', the latter more and more an independent entity, meriting its own name – 'Christianity' or 'the church'; the former light on structure, missionary in orientation, probably apocalyptic in theo-logy, the latter increasingly and perforce concerned with order and physical resources, with building community life and providing for long-term needs, and often with more speculative or quasi-philosophical styles of theology.

These various changes in the character of the Christian phenomenon, all of them readily visible to the modern observer, may well have gone unrecognized at the time, at least in anything like this analytical way, though some of them were at the root of bitter strife and controversy. It is remarked how little trace is left in the New Testament even by the Jewish rebellion of 66CE and the Fall of Jerusalem four years later, and this has been used (notably by J. A. T. Robinson, in *Redating the New Testament*) as ground for the claim that, contrary to the scholarly con-sensus, virtually all of it antedates those events. But, leaving aside the convention of referring to outward events in cryptic terms which is almost certainly in play in passages like Matt. 22.7 and Luke 19.41–44, we may suppose that gentile Christians in Greece and Asia Minor were not necessarily deeply moved by those Jewish disasters. There are indeed signs that even Jewish Christians were concerned more with the bookish, scriptural arguments with Judaism, chiefly at local level, than with events in distant Palestine, the rights and wrongs (and even the importance) of which were matters of difference among Jews themselves, as the case of Josephus indicates. If (admittedly an 'if' of uncertain power) it dates from after 70CE and is Jewish–Christian in provenance, the Letter to the Hebrews is a good indication of the over-riding role of scriptural interpretation in Christian self-understanding and self-justification in relation to Judaism and its institutions, including even the Jerusalem Temple. Indeed this style of argument was to remain standard for centuries to come.

The changes that have been described, especially the many-sided separation from Judaism, are frequently taken as both inevitable and undilutedly good, for all parties concerned. Whether from a later Christian point of view or in terms of general progress or religious clarity, these moves seem to involve a remarkable and welcome broadening out. Talk of 'emancipation from the narrow confines of Judaism' springs readily to the lips; and the theological rhetoric of Paul – about Christ as second Adam (I Cor. 15.22, 45) and about the obliteration of racial and other divisions 'in Christ' (I Cor. 12.13; Gal. 3.28) – gave a powerful impetus to such a perception virtually at the start. But from another point of view, adopted in part by pagan disparagers in the second century (see Robert L. Wilken, *The Christians as the Romans Saw Them*), the outward expansion and transformation of the Christian phenomenon, at least from Paul's mission onwards, involved a narrowing rather than a broadening, loss as well as gain.

For instance, Jews, whether approved of or not, were an identifiable, known element in the make-up of a Graeco-Roman town, recognized as having a venerable history and, in most cases, a highly distinctive way of life. They were a 'people', socially, religiously and historically. By contrast, the Christians were much more purely a religious grouping, too diverse to be identifiable in accessible terms such as those of race or class. Under one kind of lens, they had affinities with Jews (the traditional scriptures and a particular religious vocabulary); under another, they were more akin to various pagan groups, with common meals, fellowship meetings and mutual support not unlike the practice of the clubs or associations that were a familiar feature of ancient civic life. (An awareness of this difficulty – and a turning of it to advantage – is to be found in the second-century Letter to Diognetus; see Andrew Louth (ed), *Early Christian Writings*. For 'clubs', see W. A. Meeks, *The First Urban Christians*.) From an external point of view, while they claimed universality and dreamed dreams that ranged to the edges of time and space ('a new heaven and a new earth', Rev. 21.1), what they looked like was one among a great number of bizarre speculative groups which one might perhaps favour with one's interest, one option among many, with no very obvious reasons to hold one's allegiance. Their exclusiveness and rigorous demands (and from time to time their social unacceptability) would no doubt soon become apparent; but in so far as an observer brought anything like a detached, sociological eye to bear on them, they were, by comparison with Jews, a group that lacked substantial roots and cultural weight – and made extravagant and arbitrary claims. What is more, the Christians themselves were sometimes aware of this nondescript character, as the Letter to Diognetus makes plain.

Witness too Paul's reluctance to make it necessary for Christian converts of pagan background to forgo all existing social ties (I Cor. 10): only explicit involvement with pagan rites, in actuality or by implication, need be abandoned, to a large extent out of fear of giving scandal or creating a sense of religious *laissez-faire*. Partly the criterion at work was a careful discernment of what was required to avoid pollution of the Christian body (see Dale B. Martin, *The Corinthian Body*). But judgments of the care and subtlety exercised by Paul in this matter, when combined with a clear sense of the boundaries of the community 'in Christ', cannot have always made it easy to get a sense of precisely what sort of entity the church really was. But in the light of these various factors, to move from Judaism to Christianity in a Graeco-Roman city might easily appear to mean a narrowing: from a well-defined, highly distinctive entity to one stall in the socio-religious market, at first sight not all that different from (or less eccentric than) a number of others. Indeed, the profile might in certain respects look a good deal less interesting, less notable (the cult of a crucified deity!). Moreover, the life-style that was on offer was considerably less purely religious in a recognizable modern sense; that is to say, the distinctiveness of the Christians could not, like that of Jews, be seen in racial or way-of-life or quasi-political terms (Jews were often granted some rights of self-administration within a city); apart from very simple observances (baptism and eucharist – neither of them florid cultically), their distinctiveness was accessible chiefly in theological terms, especially their special beliefs about Jesus. For them, salvation lay less in an easily describable, even ostentatiously special framework of life, as in Judaism, than in inner convictions and spiritual realities not so readily visible to the outward eye; though aspects of their morality, especially their cohesive love for one another, might impress.

All the same, if they were unlike Jews in the ways described, they were unlike pagans (and like Jews) in their rejection of the cultic round that centred on the temples of every Graeco-Roman city. This was where, for all their invisibility, Christian exclusiveness (despite Paul's helpful casuistry described above) became generally apparent. From the start, this existence in a sort of no man's land alongside both Jews and pagans lent a problematic quality to the capacity of Christians to slot into their environment. It is not clear that they themselves found their apparent nondescriptness a burden, but the modern observer is bound to ask about their affinities in the civic societies of the time. Whether conscious of it or not, a new group is bound to form itself in relation to existing groups, perhaps veering towards different ones in different locations. Thus, as we have suggested, there were often similarities with the clubs which brought people together from a particular trade or locality or sharing devotion to a particular deity. Sometimes it is likely that the model was the Jewish synagogue. Especially where recruitment came from that quarter, it was the model most familiar and closest to hand. As we shall see, the Christians' adoption for their society of the word *ekklesia* ('church') may perhaps derive from its scriptural use for the 'congregation' of Israel, as a variant to *sunagoge* ('synagogue') – itself not wholly unknown among Christians of the early years (Jas. 2.2) – perhaps by way of indicating relationship-with-differentiation, in fact an accurate estimate of the situation. In other cases, the philosophical school may have contributed to the self-awareness of Christian groups: at least some of them soon developed a considerable degree of conceptual and verbal articulation (see R. Alan

Culpepper, *The Johannine School*). In the early period, it is not hard to see the Johannine congregations and some of the incipient gnostic groups having elements of this character.

Finally, in many cases it is most probable that the centring of Christian congregations on particular families meant that the urban household with its ramifications in slaves and dependants as well as close kin, was the wholly natural basis for the practical activities and the self-understanding of the group. As we shall see in various contexts, the use of domestic imagery and vocabulary sprang readily to Christian lips and pens, a good deal more than is immediately apparent in English translation. (Note for example the prominence in I Peter of words of the *oikos*, 'household', family, see J. H. Elliott, *A Home for the Homeless*.) It scarcely needs pointing out that any centring of the Christian phenomenon on particular buildings set aside uniquely for Christian use lay (as far as, say, the Pauline Christians were concerned) almost three centuries away.

Christian communities were, by the end of the first century, widely scattered and without a visible centre – a Jerusalem or a Rome. They were also, despite certain moves towards the provision of organs of codification, without uniformity in the precise terms in which they expressed their belief. No doubt there were areas of strong consensus – the lordship of Jesus and many of the words in which this was expressed, his saving efficacy, the use of baptism, the observance of eucharist – but there were varieties of idiom and different 'families' or clusters of Christian communities, whether those of a particular area or those that owed their origin to a particular missionary or his associates: hence we can speak of Pauline or Johannine churches, and note the seven churches addressed, as in some way pastorally dependent, by the seer of the Revelation of John.

Yet there was also a sense of membership of a common and single entity and of engagement in a common endeavour under a single lordship. What held this disparate entity together? Earlier, I referred to it as a network. The lines of its cohesion were, it seems, chiefly visits and writings. There is strong evidence for both in the New Testament itself (notably in the letters included there), and remarkable physical testimony to the rapid and far-reaching spread of documents in the survival of second- and third-century papyri in even quite remote parts of Egypt, far from the places of origin of the New Testament (and other) writings of which they are copies (see C. H. Roberts, *Manuscript, Society and Belief in Early Christian Egypt*, and G. N. Stanton, *Gospel Truth? New Light on Jesus and the Gospels*). The network was highly effective and itself contributed to the intensity of Christian self-awareness and devotion of which it was itself a major expression (see Larry W. Hurtado, *One God, One Lord*). These flourishing contacts kept alive and well the memory of Jesus and the visions of present life and future glory that he inspired and made possible.

Was the Church Inevitable?

Before we turn to the thought of the New Testament writers themselves on the subject of the Christian community, it may be worthwhile standing back a little to consider the necessity of the church. This means looking at some of the matters already referred to from a different angle.

A television programme on how the church deals with change ended with a refreshing aphorism from Kenneth Leech: 'Christianity is very simple. All it requires is a memory and a vision; and, if it can get them, some bread and wine, and water.' You do not have to unpack that statement very far to find yourself back in the wrangles from which, in the television programme, it effected a timely rescue. All the same, it serves a useful purpose in drawing attention to one dimension of, perhaps, any faith: its essential directness and underlying simplicity. Without those qualities it can scarcely attract or operate, whatever the subtleties and complexities that are superadded in its life and thought. However, the statement omits, or rather skates over (or perhaps presupposes), one vital factor – that which in fact generally presents itself first of all to believers and non-believers alike: the Christian church, as the community or institution in which, through time and space, the memory is held, the vision is captured, and the bread, wine and water are used to encapsulate and focus both beliefs and commitment in the rites of eucharist and baptism.

Now the church (however it presents itself) is so much a fact of life – for Christians of all kinds and, in many parts of the world, for society in general – that there seems something almost perverse in raising the question of its appropriateness in the religion that stems from and centres on Jesus of Nazareth. There is of course an immediate, impatient and commonsense response to any such questioning: How do you think Jesus of Nazareth could have had any lasting influence if there had not come into being a body of believers sufficiently cohesive to present him as master and teacher to successive generations? The answer is not quite as clear as the impatience of the question suggests. Even if we confine ourselves to European culture, there have been figures of immense and long-lasting influence (Plato, Aristotle) where there has been no succeeding apparatus at all comparable to that of the church: their books and a succession of expositors have sufficed. Of course great philosophers play a different, less all-embracing role in the perception of their followers than Jesus in the perception of Christians. They are not the recipients of worship, not often seen as living presences and directors of their followers' whole lives; and their adherents do not as a rule (though there have been short-term and small-scale exceptions) reckon to share a close-knit community life. Though in one respect they have greater potency than Jesus, in that their teachings are more directly available in black and white than his, which exist only by the mediation of the selection and thought-processes of the evangelists. And, to go further, there have been whole tracts of Christian history when, at the level of sophisticated formulation, those ancient philosophers have so dominated the shape of Christian minds that, in this particular aspect of the Christian religion and for those appropriately trained, they may be said to have gone far to commandeer the Christian enterprise, to have incorporated Jesus into their system. It is possible to have a lively discussion on whether the reverse is not a better account of things – that is, that the Jesus-centred faith used the philosophers, at different times, as convenient tools for its self-expression, remaining itself distinctive and immune at the core and moulding their teaching to its own essential features; but the former perspective is not without its plausibility.

Be that as it may, the omnipresence of the church over so many centuries makes it hard to go back in imagination to the beginning and ask whether there is not something surprising about the fact that the movement stemming from Jesus gave rise to an entity such as the church. The question is of more than antiquarian interest and other than idle speculation, not just for Christians who feel impelled to attend to origins for edification if not necessarily for imitation, but also because if there were 'non-church' forces at work in the earliest days, these may (given that the imprint of that time survives in the New Testament) have created a continuing, ineradicable tension with the 'church' forces whose dominance has been so complete: they may have put permanent grit in the machine, created a lasting awkwardness, so that the church might not ever be wholly at ease with itself and have an element in its consciousness that might make it feel, in a certain sense, uncomfortable in being there at all! Historical evidence for such unease abounds, of course, in the reform movements in Christianity, though, while they have usually rejected the church as it currently projected itself, have not generally questioned the very notion of the church as an appropriate expression of Christian faith.

To go back to the beginning: were there elements in the work of Jesus himself that militated against the very notion of such a thing as 'church', that is, an organized community of adherents? Any answer to this question is made tentative and uncertain by the difficulty of assessing the evidence of the gospels (as we shall see more specifically in later chapters). We cannot tell (despite the many confident attempts) how far and in what respects the depiction of Jesus which they contain, itself different in each of the four, reflects features of Christian life and belief operating in the period between Jesus and the evangelist and in the thought of the evangelist himself, rather than the realities of Jesus' own life. With regard to our present subject, the question is whether the undoubted existence of Christian communities in the subsequent decades has coloured the portrayal of the life-time of Jesus, when they did not then exist at all and were perhaps inimical to his whole purpose and strategy. As we shall consider this matter in more detail later, it is now necessary only to establish the shape of the question and to make plain that it admits of no easy or final answer.

That 'shape' is further complicated by ambiguities in the connotation of 'church' itself. Even when we have successfully stripped off later associations and freed ourselves of anachronism, we may encounter four possible kinds of awareness in early Christianity in relation to the corporate expression of the Christian movement. There can first be awareness of Christian community as embodied essentially in the congregation to which one belongs. Even if one knows perfectly well that there are other similar groups and even if there is contact with them from time to time, it is natural, especially when distances are great and communications meagre, for one's whole practical horizon to be filled by one's own Christian group. So it must have been for most members of the first-century churches. Or else there can be primary awareness of the Christian movement as a whole, with one's own group as an element within the greater totality. Such awareness would be expected in missionaries or leaders who visited groups other than their own, perhaps as delegates for some common purpose. And either of these styles may exist at a practical, matter-of-fact level ('we are Christians who group together for certain convenient purposes') or at a level of high theory, where beliefs are held about the community itself that are integrated with basic Christian convictions. In other words, in relation to both local and universal levels, there may exist both a non-theological and a theological sense of the matter. As all four kinds of awareness persist in the present within Christianity in various forms, there is no great difficulty in envisioning them. Though they are not always easy to identify, all four seem to be present in early Christianity; and of course, the modern theological counterparts (and in some circumstances there can be a theological justification of the non-theological styles of church awareness!) owe much to models discerned in the New Testament itself.

Given that the gospels are inherently problematic, because of their late date and church provenance, it may seem sensible to look for contemporary parallels to the Jesus-movement itself. Are there comparable movements in Judaism that may shed light on that led by Jesus? In recent years a variety of candidates have been advanced, the Qumran community, Cynic philosophers, and more shadowy apocalyptic nationalist groups being the most common (see John P. Meier, *A Marginal Jew*; J.D. Crossan, *The Historical Jesus*, and *Jesus, A Revolutionary Biography*). But much the best candidate for comparison is that suggested by the gospels themselves, John the Baptist.

Unfortunately, however, his case raises many of the same questions as that of Jesus himself when it comes to the matter of a lasting expression in community form, whatever differences and similarities there may have been in the tone and content of their messages. For all that, if Jesus had close associates, so did John (e.g. Matt. 11.2ff.). In both cases there is the question how far those associates saw themselves as *ad hoc* helpers in a short-term campaign, looking towards an imminent transformation of the world by God and urging readiness for that coming 'kingdom' and the judgment it would entail, and how far as prospective leaders in some kind of community within the new order. In both cases, there is little sign that in the lifetime of the great teachers there was a concern to establish formal groups of adherents beyond the helpers themselves: the absence of any such element in the instructions for missionary work in the gospels (Mark 6.1–6 and parallels in Matt. 10 and Luke 9; 10) seems, in the case of Jesus, to have a strong claim to historical accuracy: there was after all an incentive to 'read back' more formal arrangements into Jesus' life-time and claim his authority for them – we probably see this tendency at work in the material on church discipline in Matt. 18.15ff. Nevertheless, other interpretations are possible: the mission instructions may represent just one aspect among others (i.e. the missionary as opposed to the 'church maintenance' or disciplinary side) of church operations in the later first century; or (perhaps less likely – but it is not fruitless to have a sense of the range of possibilities and so of the intractability of our sources) a kind of idealization, a picture of what (it was felt) should have been and no longer was – in effect the earliest case of anti-institutional bias, seeking to erase from Christian memory Jesus' own steps towards the now-regretted institutionalizing of his followers.

Against this is the readiness of Matthew particularly to incorporate material of a 'proto-institutional' kind, as we have seen (see also 16.17–19; 19.28). It is, after all, uncertain whether the Twelve (assuming their historicity, despite some diversity among the lists of their names given in Mark, Matthew, Luke and Acts) speak for organization among Jesus' followers here and now or merely look forward to an as-yet-unformed renewed people of God, a purified and restored Israel in the coming new dispensation, of which, in the meantime, they were a living icon.

Finally, whatever was true in the life-time of both John and Jesus and whatever their intentions for the future, it is clear that not only Jesus but also John gave rise to movements that did survive their life-time. In the case of the followers of John, we cannot tell how far there was a parallel to the church in terms of formality or elaboration, but at least, according to Acts (18.24–19.6), they were capable of movement as a group to Asia Minor, though their purpose there is not disclosed; and, on a reading of the Gospel of John that sees it as throwing light on the Johannine church's own setting, they were a group able to interact, in some unidentifiable way, with that church as a parallel group (John 3.22–4.3; and see R. E. Brown, *The Community of the Beloved Disciple*). Historically speaking, the enigmatic disciples of John the Baptist in Acts may even represent a stage when the two prophetic movements were not differentiated as clearly as they soon came to be (see Jerome Murphy-O'Connor, *Paul, A Critical Life*). In essence, while the church that emerges as the formalization of the Jesus-movement is unique in its eventual development, it is unclear whether or how far it represents a distortion of elements in the intentions and activities of Jesus himself.

Those intentions are themselves difficult to 'read', and there are at least three major possibilities, each carrying implications for our sense of the community dimension. First, supposing we see Jesus (like John the Baptist in many respects) as leading a 'reform movement in Judaism', then, apart from his group of helpers, the Twelve, there is little sign of his establishing a cohesive body of followers (but see Luke 8.1–3 and Mark 15.40f. for the women in Jesus' entourage, whose position in the itinerant mission movement is scarcely definable on the scant evidence before us) – more an attentive audience with its varied degrees of receptiveness, with some individuals the beneficiaries of his healing. Not much in the Gospels encourages us to think that Jesus set about establishing local guilds of enthusiasts, such as the Pharisees seem to have been in relation to the Torah. It appears that reform was, at least initially, to be a matter of individual and inward conviction and resolve – and of readiness for the revelation of God's consummation. Second, supposing the doctrine of this reform movement was apocalyptic in its chief emphasis, even then (as I have already hinted) the place of a communal dimension remains unsettled. On all the parallels in contemporary Judaism, the future hope would centre on a strong sense of a renewed and faithful people of God, whether purely Jewish or also including righteous gentiles, but how far such a people might be expected to organize itself formally in the meantime, a kind of Israel-within-Israel, remains open. The example of Qumran speaks strongly in favour of such organization, but in its strength, solidity and durability it seems to be unique and by no means rules out the possibility of other models. If the Jesus-movement were chiefly apocalyptic in orientation (and it is highly unlikely that this dimension was absent or even subordinate), then the Gospel teaching

on behaviour in the present world-order, so prominent
especially in Matthew and Luke, may (though not at all
necessarily – the meticulous regulation of life at Qumran
suggests otherwise) be seen as the provision of the church
for its own needs in the ever-lengthening interim, and as
fathered on Jesus as the fount of all truth and authority.
But third, if the teaching of Jesus bearing on conduct in
this world, some of it radical, some homely and prudent
wisdom, in fact were to be taken as representing histori-
cally the main thrust of his provision for his followers and
his audiences, then the question of his envisaging a community is still not easily settled. Taken as a whole, that
teaching certainly includes material which has a community in mind (e.g. Matt. 18), but much of it is perfectly
capable of being taken as moral inspiration and guidance
for the individual, as many modern, non-church admirers
of Jesus are apt to testify.

There is in any case reason to suppose that, however
odd it may seem in strict logic, apocalyptic vision and
detailed this-worldly moral concern can perfectly well
have co-existed, as the example of Qumran demonstrates.
And even though, in that case, community necessity gave
the context and the spur for provision for the present, it is
not hard to imagine a need for it in other, less strongly
communal circumstances, even those of the circle around
Jesus. Though the urban context no doubt makes a great
difference from the rural setting and largely itinerant
character of Jesus' activity, it is after all the case that Paul's
outlook combined apocalyptic vision and moral guidance,
not all of which (e.g. Rom. 12) is conditioned by the
perspective of an imminent transformation of all things –
though that outcome is in view in the very next passage
(Rom. 13.11). Paul found it possible to live intellectually
as well as practically in both dimensions, to discourse

seriously about both, and even to let the two interact in ways that do not always seem fully convincing: while his teaching on marriage cases in I Cor. 7 takes sensible account of the effects of an imminent upturning of present commitments and arrangements, it is natural to question (though one may also understand the impulse behind it) his teaching on tax-paying in Rom. 13 (if genuinely his) which surely envisages a settled existence for the imperial order.

Enough has been said about what I described as a discomfort inherent in the very notion of 'church', a discomfort still manifesting itself in a wide variety of forms: the regular dissatisfaction of Christians with the infidelities of the church to the vision and teaching of Jesus; the constant oscillations between protest and accommodation in the church's relationship with society and the state; the uncertainties about the individual's relation to the Christian community, especially the extent to which commitment, even absorption, may rightly be demanded and given; the degree to which raising a banner for the otherworldly or spiritual dimension entails rejection of worldly and material concerns and opportunities, crucially in the areas of family and property (alternately disturbers and comforters of the Christian conscience). All these perennial uncertainties are already visible, though in embryo, in the standpoints adopted by the various New Testament writers in relation to the corporate ongoing expression of Christian commitment.

As we shall see, other issues, whose modern resonances are more indirect, often loomed larger in this regard in these early years, notably the relation between on the one hand the rootedness of Jesus and the church not only in a Jewish context but also in a Jewish past, and on the other hand the novelty of his teaching and his role on God's behalf. This ambiguity has its later counterparts in the church's harmony and disharmony with society at large, with its own institutions and traditions, and with its setting in history; but the original form of it, though a matter very much of those first years, has continued to resonate in the anguished and controverted subject of Christianity's relation to Judaism at successive stages of the continually developing life of the two faiths.

It is time now to turn to some of the early Christian writers in order to see how they dealt with the matter of the Christian community and what beliefs they held about this entity which was the increasingly independent and identifiable visible embodiment of response to Jesus and adherence to his cause.

2

Paul on the Church

Though I have now used the term 'church' a number of times in this book, it has always been with a certain inner reluctance, and I have often preferred to speak of 'the Christian community' or, rather cumbersomely, 'the communal or corporate dimension of Christianity' or 'Christian congregations'. All these expressions have their drawbacks, their misleading resonances, but they often have the edge over 'church' because that term has so many more. In turning to the thought of Paul about the Christian community, there is no alternative to facing the difficulty head on, and indeed elucidating it; for Paul, the very first Christian writer available to us, uses the word *ekklesia*, normally rendered 'church', with greater frequency than any other early Christian writer (62 out of 114 occurrences in the whole New Testament) – though of course his material is of such a character that that is not necessarily remarkable, when it is put alongside the Gospels, for example; but at least it shows the word was no neologism in late first-century Christian usage, for Paul uses it with entire naturalness. Whether it was Paul's innovation we cannot tell, but he gives no sign that it needed explaining to those he wrote to, and there is no denying that by the time of his letters, that is by the fifties, when the greater part of his missionary work in founding Christian groups was already accomplished, this was the word by which those groups were normally described.

Yet the use of 'church' by us demands caution simply because so many of its modern associations are inapplicable. It is a difficulty we encounter similarly when, in the context of New Testament Christianity, we use for Christian leaders and officers words like 'bishop', 'deacon', or 'minister' which had not then acquired Christian technicality and whose later connotations are so different, so overladen. We are in territory where anachronism prowls at will and often finds a ready welcome. Now, 'church' signifies most commonly either a building set aside for Christian worship or the great ecclesiastical institution in one of its forms, as in expressions like 'the church affirms' and 'church and state'. Whatever the historical institutional continuity of the Christian society between then and now, neither of these dominant modern senses has any place in the usage of the New Testament or the realities behind it; and however much theological or emotional store is set by continuity, discontinuity is equally striking and significant (see Robert L. Wilken, *The Myth of Christian Beginnings*).

Ekklesia signifies most commonly in the New Testament's usage the local Christian group, especially when gathered together – in realistic terms, anything from perhaps a dozen to fifty people: Paul seems to feel that it is most itself when concentrated in one place for its common purposes, or even that Christians are most themselves when physically together (see Robert Banks, *Paul's Idea of Community*). In I Cor. 11.22, Paul's view seems to be that a higher standard of Christian mutuality and equality is required at the Christian meeting than can be expected in the privacy of the home; and, incidentally, it makes an interesting reversal of the common modern exhortation to take Christian dispositions out into daily life! This focussing on the meeting of the Christian group as the

most intense and in that sense normative expression of
Christian 'being' is implicit in the underlying sense and use
of *ekklesia*: it signifies an assembly, commonly and most
familiarly that of the free citizens of a Greek city (see Acts
19.32, 39, 41) and, in a few examples, the meetings for
business of the clubs which may have been one, partial
model or point of reference for the Christian groups on the
social map of the cities of the Eastern Mediterranean. But
we have no way of telling how far Paul's favouring of the
word (and perhaps even his originating of it as the
standard term for the Christian groups) derived from
either of these examples. Civic metaphors for Christian life
do not abound in Paul's thought, Phil. 3.20 offering the
only substantial instance. And the fact that much the
commonest use of it in Paul's undoubted letters refers to
the individual Christian congregation and not to the
Christian movement as a whole (though see I Cor.
10.32 and probably 12.28, apostles being largely 'supra'-
congregational figures) speaks against the citizen assembly
as the dominant model.

His ready and frequent use of the word may, however,
have come from its use in the Septuagint as one rendering
of *qahal*, to refer to the 'congregation' of Israel: each
group is a sort of epitome of the whole. But again, Paul
does not draw attention to this source, for example by
quoting or even alluding plainly to scriptural passages
that use it. And, if this is the source, why did he prefer
this word to the much more common *sunagoge*? Not surprisingly, it is suggested that it reflects a deliberate
differentiation in terms of basic vocabulary from the
Jewish gatherings in the Hellenistic world that had
adopted this Greek word for themselves. But it is not clear
how general the term (or indeed the formal institution)
was already among Jews of Paul's day; nor does it seem

that Paul's sense of Christian differentiation from Judaism was keen enough to warrant distinctive, rather defiant nomenclature, or indeed that he regularly saw himself as belonging to a distinct institution at all. Only passing statements like I Cor. 10.32, significant as they are, point this way. Generally, he is keener to assert essential authenticity in 'Israel' terms for the Christian movement and mission (Rom. 9–11; Gal. 6.16). It is, however, conceivable that the use of this distinctive term did reflect a sense of discomfort and rejection inflicted in certain places by Jews' suspicion of the Christian groups, or of gentile Christians' reluctance to be seen as lumped together with the often unpopular and 'weird' Jewish gatherings. For them, it was one thing to worship Jesus as 'lord', a figure presented as transcending his earthly Jewishness; quite another to be made to feel, in the very name for your group, somehow a close relation of the Jewish community – who were anyway not keen to adopt you. Deeply reluctant though Paul was to admit decisive distance from that community for himself, nevertheless gentile converts to the Pauline gospel, bound to none of the essential marks of Jewish racial and religious identity (and so thoroughly eccentric, at the very least, from a Jewish point of view), would doubtless feel easier with a self-description which put a gap between the two groups, while not indicating total rupture, and which resonated somewhat with their secular life. In many ways, the simplest and most satisfactory solution is that Paul was ready to use *ekklesia* in its most ordinary and non-ideological associations. What are you joining? We are joining 'the group'. Parallels abound; and the capital initial letter can be trusted to grow of its own accord in such cases.

If we move out from the somewhat mysterious adoption by Paul, if not by others before him, of this word as normal for the Christian community, we find that reflection about the rationale of this new (but how new exactly?) entity is, in Paul's thought, deeply conditioned by the question of standing in relation to Judaism, whether the use of *ekklesia* has much to do with the matter or not. Moreover, his own thought exemplifies that ambiguity of attitude to Judaism which, on one line of argument suggested above, may have played a part in making this word an acceptable self-designation for the Christian groups. Only now, the ambiguity involves more than the assimilation and social comfort of gentile adherents. It is a question of Paul's whole perception of God's purpose in history as scripturally warranted, and it is a matter occasioning the utmost anguish. This arises not from ordinary hesitation and indecision but from rival and, in his scheme of things, irreconcilable convictions, held at the deepest level of his being and undeniable because of his most profound experience. We shall see that there were factors that disguised the conflict between the different components of his outlook, even from Paul himself, but they served less to ease the tensions than to blur their candid recognition.

The essential question can be simply stated: was Christianity new? Much spoke for the answer Yes: the very existence and force of the new movement (it was a fresh feature on the social scene) and the high claims made for Jesus pointed unequivocally this way, all the more in the predominantly gentile setting of Graeco-Roman towns. But you have only to turn to deep convictions about the God to whom Jesus relates as 'son' to 'father', and to that God's age-old and identifiable relationship with the world in general and Israel in particular, through whom his character is articulated; only to feel the need for bearings and landmarks in terms of arguments and vocabulary to legitimate and give body to the community's life; only to utter almost any of the Christian words; for a negative answer of some kind then to impose itself.

With regard to the Christian phenomenon as a whole, as both belief and institution, early Christianity offered almost every possible answer to the question of its status in relation to what went before. The relationship to Judaism is one of wholesale rejection; or else it is one of utmost continuity; or of fulfilment; or of supersession; or of building on well-loved foundations; or of kicking them aside. At the level of theory, and from time to time with practical implications of the utmost gravity, it is of course the case that all these positions have persisted in Christianity, taking new forms in changing historical situations. The difficulty with Paul is that his mind contains elements of all of them, and is able to hold all the disparate elements with passion. In this respect (as in others), he is the father of a brood of incompatible tendencies in Christianity, able to be claimed by all with varying degrees of plausibility and anachronism. He managed to harbour them all in a single human experience: his progeny have found it more natural to bring their differences into the open, whatever eirenic formulas may be found to diminish them. In the case of Paul himself, such is his vehemence and clarity in expressing a number of distinct visions that to submit them to any such process is to falsify them or to blunt their edge.

In the first place, Paul sees the strongest continuity between Israel and the church. This is probably (if briefly) expressed in the reference to the priority of Jew over Greek in the word 'first' in Rom. 1.16 – whether that priority be temporal or qualitative; and it is worked out at length in the argument of Rom. 9–11. If those chapters are to be taken as the climax of the main argument of Romans, outlining the historical dénouement to which, in the end,

Christ's saving work leads (and not as a speculative appendage to a theology of personal salvation), then they testify forcefully to Paul's sense of the church's essential continuity with Israel and as now the bearer, and certainly not the extinguisher, of Israel's God-given purpose and hope. It is true that this role, assigned to the gentile church and audaciously making it the pioneer and exemplar of the completion of Israel's own destiny, represents a major turn-about from the Jewish sense of the future, in which gentiles might at best play a subordinate role; but it is still a scheme in which the two entities, while distinguishable, are bound together in a single ultimate community and as instruments of a single purpose, actors in a single divine drama, enfolding all and greater than all. It is not so much that the church 'fulfils' what has been laid down or fore-seen in the Jewish past (the word occurs in Paul but not frequently and not properly in this sense); more that it is part and parcel of the Jewish story and, now, in its gentile manifestation specifically, the bearer of Israel's hope. Only once (see Gal. 6.16) does this picture issue in what seems to be the idea of the church as itself 'Israel', a reference that stands, in equal isolation, at the opposite end of a spectrum from I Cor. 10.32 where the church is wholly distinguished from both Jews and Greeks, a third entity within the human race.

Rom. 9.1–5 shows how the join between Jews and gentiles is understood. Jesus himself, as Israel's Messiah (Rom. 9.5 is one of the very few cases of Paul using the word *christos* in its technical sense and with technical force, as if placing himself on Jewish ground) is the link, but here Jesus himself is assimilated to a rich list of essen-tial features of Israel's beneficent endowment at God's hands. Thus, in terms of cold logic, Paul here treats Jesus as, however crucial, but one incident or feature, alongside

many others, in Israel's providential story. The divinely
guided story is the essence of the matter; Jesus is that agent
within it who triggers off its final stages – the process
where, by way of his becoming a bone of contention,
gentiles are embraced by Israel's God into communal relationship with him and, in Paul's belief, will win the Jews,
by emulation, to the messianic banner (now seen as in
Jesus' hands) and so to acceptance of the fruits of the
divine plan.

It is hard to imagine a stronger contrast than that
between this model, in effect subordinating Christ to the
historical process that contains him even as it leads to him
and gives him the crucial role, and that which sees Christ
as the bearer and initiator of a new beginning to creation
itself. Paul sees him as a counterpart to Adam, but one free
from the mortal legacy bequeathed by him – counterpart
not simply heir (Rom. 5.12ff.; I Cor. 15.22, 45); and his
adherents (those 'in him') as participating in no less than a
new creation (II Cor. 5.17; Gal. 6.15) – thus fulfilling in
radical manner the most far-reaching apocalyptic hopes,
apparently within (rather than simply subsequent to) the
present world-order, 'passing away' as that order is (I Cor.
7.31). It is a claim of the utmost audacity. While the
notion of a renewal of the created order is an element in
some patterns of Jewish apocalyptic hope (with scriptural
passages like Isa. 11.6–9 and 65.17 for background and
spur), it is a new step to attach it to a historical figure and
the movement he inaugurates. This claim, with its use of
the symbol of Adam who transcends as well as antedates
the division of the human race into Jews and gentiles,
carries the implication of radical discontinuity at the point
of Christ. By its logic, any need to place Christ in the
sequence of Israel's story is rendered otiose, as is the
need for a strategy whereby gentiles and Jews can be

brought together in God's people – such as Rom. 9–11 so elaborately proposes. Rather, Christ has the effect of simply annulling the distinction between Jews and gentiles, as indeed he removes distinctions of social station and of gender (Gal. 3.28). What these claims signified in the day-to-day life of Paul's congregations and what was the extent of their practical effectiveness (was it a function of the sense that the church was most intensely itself when meeting together?) is not our immediate concern. The fact is that they bespeak a model for thinking of the church whose logic runs counter to that which places Jesus within the historical process, an item or episode (however crucial) in God's dealings with his people. According to this second model, the figure of Christ simply by-passes or transcends any ultimate specialness that might be thought to attach to Israel and entails the equality of all in relation to God. His appearing in the world (admittedly in a Jewish setting, Gal. 4.4), with its promise of imminent triumphant consummation, is a genuine novum. At that point, there is discontinuity not only with the past but, as we have seen, with contemporary social structures. In Paul's vision of things, all the markers of personal identity (social, familial, racial and sexual) are relativized and even subsumed by the single identity-marker: Christ and the shared life 'in him'. This is Paul as revolutionary.

In this pattern, Adam does not really function as a historical figure, the inaugurator of the race centuries and centuries before, with those centuries stretching out in the imagination as they are likely to do for modern temporally minded readers of Paul, attempting to share his mind. Though of course in part a figure in the past, Adam is much more a figure in scripture and a symbol that provides bearings, a point of reference for understanding the significance of Jesus. According to this model, understanding Jesus does not quite 'require' Adam, in the way that the former model 'requires' Israel and its story. Jesus is the direct, unexpected gift from God – 'the man from heaven' (I Cor. 15.47); and Adam makes a striking, scripturally provided indicator of his importance, above all of his universality with regard to the human race, but the claim could have been made without recourse to him.

Now, Paul shows no sign of fretting under the strain of working with two incompatible models for understanding the Christian community's place in the world: as having its essential role in relation to Israel, or else as free-standing, the pioneer of the new human race, its meaning wholly determined by the meaning of Christ. While this might seem surprising to us, it is not inexplicable, and there were theological conventions on hand that would conceal and even seem to remove the risk of incompatibility. But the phrase 'theological conventions' is false: like the perception of incompatibility itself, it assumes a modern standpoint at a distance from Paul's own and it carries a misleading impression of conscious contrivance. For him, two loyalties were absolute and both were constitutive of his identity: to Jewishness and to Christ. Neither was negotiable, intellectually or emotionally, as passages like Rom. 9.1–5 on the one hand and Gal. 2.20 on the other, demonstrate: Jesus was Messiah of Israel, yes, but he was also the one who 'loved me and gave himself for me'. It is well established that in the ancient world a person's sense of identity was usually not so much the outcome of a process of personal exploration and development as the effect of participation in the group or groups to which one belonged (see, for example, Bruce J. Malina and Jerome H. Neyrey, 'First-century Personality: Dyadic not Individual', in Neyrey (ed), *The Social World of Luke-Acts*). It is therefore not in the least surprising that Paul's sense of Christ's call should issue so directly and intensely in a sense of the Christian community as wholly bound up with him ('in Christ'), with its identity dependent on him, rather than as, say, a society of persons interested in Christ's career or teaching. Nor is it surprising that, especially at this very early stage of Christian reflection, Paul seems to have felt no pressure towards a formal reconciliation of the two disparate tendencies: continuity furthered and discontinuity asserted at the self-same point, that of Christ's irruption on to the scene.

But (to resume) the contrariety was disguised by certain equally well embedded elements in Paul's mental equipment, notably various aspects of scriptural prophecy: figures, statements and concepts in the scriptures that were seen as pointing to Christ and both explicating and determining his role. We may be inclined to see these as serviceable images that illuminate the person and story of Jesus, even as normative icons which, in the historical context, were essential if he were to be intelligible, and without which he would have existed in a kind of void, a bolt from the blue (indeed, 'the man from heaven'!) without bearings in the human world.

One of these images has already been encountered in relation to its role in enabling Paul to go beyond the picture of Jesus as enclosed within the Jewish story: the figure of Adam. While Adam is indeed effective conceptually in achieving that end (he signifies humanity as a whole, of all times and places, and the Adam icon enables Jesus to be seen as 'second Adam', a brand new start for everybody), he is also a figure in scripture, the first human actor in the very story he enables Paul to transcend. Hence both his great effectiveness in Paul's total theological picture and his contribution to a blurring of the two models between which I have distinguished.

It is somewhat similar with the figure of Abraham. In a passage like Rom. 11.1, he is simply the ancestor – a crucial figure back in Israel's story, into which gentiles have been incorporated. But in Rom. 4, he appears in a quite different role – as an icon of justification by faith and so as a kind of crypto-Christian, a Christian *avant la lettre*, seen not so much as a figure of long ago, a providential freak living centuries before the full establishment of that relation to God that he anticipated and foreshadowed, but as a scriptural (and so authoritative) example, legitimating the true mode of relationship with God and establishing it at the roots of Jewishness in the very words associated with him in Gen. 15.6 (together with other texts). In Gal. 3, his role is again primarily iconic and scriptural, while put in a formally historical argument about Abraham's true inheritance: as the one whose true 'seed' Christ is (Gen. 13.15).

Moreover, in so far as (and it is not prominent in Paul) Christ is seen as pre-existent, himself operative, perhaps through identification with God's 'wisdom' (I Cor. 1.24), in creation (I Cor. 8.6) and in scriptural episodes (I Cor. 10.4), he himself blurs the distinction between continuity and discontinuity at the point of his appearance in the world: he was there all along! Though again, the sense is probably that he is 'in the book' rather than that he was 'in the past'.

Finally, there are traces in Paul of the idea of a kind of parallelism between the Jewish scriptural dispensation and that associated with Christ. Undoubtedly, this picture of things leans towards the model of discontinuity – a new state of affairs has now arrived – yet, when strictly applied, its newness is constrained by the felt need to replicate in the new set-up the features, concepts and institutions of the old. There are elements of this approach in I Cor. 10.1–13, where parallels to baptism and eucharist are discerned in the wilderness story of Exodus, and perhaps in the application to Christians and the church of the image of the temple (I Cor. 3.16; 6.19). But in these cases, the feeling is that the new Christian phenomena are calling the tune: it is not a question of a painstaking sense of obligation to reproduce in the new the full paraphernalia of the old, such as was later felt in the importation into eucharistic liturgy and priestly accoutrements of ideas and equipment from the Levitical sacrifices, or indeed in the widespread belief in Christian countries that because the Israel of the Old Testament lived under a monarchy, so should Christian nations. (The coronation rites of European tradition are heavily dependent on such an ideology.) But something of this stronger development of typology along these lines can be seen in the parallel between old and new covenants in II Cor. 3, though contrast is as much to the fore as comparison (see the much more developed form of this theme in the Letter to the Hebrews).

All these factors serve in Paul, and in subsequent times, to create a certain mist over the question of the nature of the church, loading it with a persisting ambiguity in its relation to Judaism. Focussing on the model of continuity, we may say that it is one thing to recognize the plain fact that Jesus appears in a Jewish setting and that the origins of the church lie, in the opening years at any rate, in Judaism, however rapidly it was subject to other influences and however idiosyncratic the way Judaism was interpreted by a figure like Paul; but it is quite another to give to this historical circumstance particular – and permanent – theological force; for example, with the claim that there is a continuing special relationship in God's providence between Judaism and Christianity (whatever the transforming developments to which both have been subject

down the years). After all, in the terms of his model of discontinuity, Paul did everything he could to dismiss any
such doctrine: in Christ 'there is neither Jew nor Greek'
(Gal. 3.28): reading that, one would never guess at the
anguish revealed in Rom. 9–11 and the speculative and
unrealized process there envisaged towards an end – which
here is simply given 'in Christ'. It was (just) possible – for
local and particular reasons to do with his own situation
and his mode of reading scripture – for Paul to work with
these conflicting tendencies; not so easy for successors in
quite different settings of both life and thought. Yet the
legacy still dogs inter-religious relations; which might
profit from a little clarification of Paul's ambiguous
bequest along these lines.

If Paul's model of continuity focusses on the story of
Israel, its scriptural past and its speculative future, his
model of discontinuity, which is his dominant Christian
legacy, is expressed in a number of semi-independent
images, each shedding light in one way or another on the
newness and the Christ-dependence and Christ-centred-
ness of the Christian community. It is interesting that
Paul's basic term for that community, 'the church', is alone
in not springing from this model; as we have seen, it either
belongs to the Israel picture or is relatively colourless in its
associations – Paul never explains it. There is some irony
in the thought that the term whose elucidation has been
the source of such strife down the centuries may well have
started its Christian career as innocently as could possibly
be – if it is innocent to signify very little.

Much the most striking of the images Paul employs to
give expression to his sense of the Christian community as
depending solely on Christ – and on no superior or
anterior entity, save God himself – 'church *of God*', Gal.
1.13; 'churches *of Christ*', 1.22) is that of the body. Its

provenance is disputed: is it the established use of the metaphor of the parts of the human body for the relation of citizens to the state or community in which they live – in which case Paul subverts its hierarchical application with his promotion of the powerless in I Cor. 12 (see Dale B. Martin, *The Corinthian Body*)? Or is it perhaps stimulated by the familiar sight at pagan temples of models of human limbs, testifying to healings experienced there under the auspices of the relevant god (see Jerome Murphy-O'Connor, *Paul, A Critical Life*)? But whatever its origin, it proved capable in Paul's hands not only of startling adaptation to the matter of shared relationship with the person of Christ, but also of almost chameleon-like adjustment to a variety of ideas which Paul wished to communicate to his readers. It is best seen as a general reservoir of imagery on which Paul draws for a number of purposes.

The most extensive application is however to the local congregation, in particular the Christian community in Corinth. In that respect, it marches alongside the use of *ekklesia* (and, like *ekklesia*, it was to move out later, and apparently effortlessly, into application to the universal Christian community, notably in Colossians and in the probably pseudonymous Ephesians). The need of that particular congregation to be taught a lesson about mutual respect and esteem among its members was well met in the picture of a body's parts all being necessary to the smooth functioning of the whole: varied gifts and roles are to collaborate and not compete, and, more importantly, those of higher social status are not to dominate or despise their fellow-Christians of more humble standing (I Cor. 12).

Yet the way in which the image first appears in the letter suggests that a source other than the two referred to above makes a substantial contribution to its use. It is the presence of the idea of Jesus' body in the tradition of the Last Supper and so in a story that, for Paul at least, was central to the observance of the common eucharistic meal. Paul told that story, including Jesus' words in relation to the bread, 'This is my body, which is for your sakes', in 11.23–25; a formula which itself links the gathered Christian group intimately with Jesus. And earlier still, in 10.16f., Paul has made the same connections, this time putting the theme in even stronger, causal terms: 'because there is one loaf, we, many as we are, are one body, for we all share in the one loaf'. Both the outer clauses in this sentence state the causal relationship between shared loaf and common participation in the 'body'. The central Christian observance of the eucharistic meal impressed itself on Paul's mind and stimulated the linking of the bread and those who received it, both of them expressive of Christ. But Paul's use of the idea in I Cor. 12, while following easily from the injunctions about conduct at the common meal in the preceding chapter, is determined chiefly by the pressing need to deal with the aggressive spiritual tactics of the socially dominant members of the congregation. He is concerned to undermine their hegemony by a concrete appeal to the fact of Christ's self-giving, sacrifice contrasting with assertion, radical humility with dominance.

The 'body' image is flexible, however, and Paul is not wedded to this corporate use of it which has become so influential in later Christian doctrinal thinking about the church. In I Cor. 6.12ff., the main focus is on the bond between the individual and Christ, and in I Cor. 15, with its extended discussion of the role of bodies in the fulfilled resurrection world, the thought is again of individual Christians, existing as distinct Spirit-formed and Spirit-driven bodies, with the risen and heavenly Christ as the pioneer and guarantor of this blessed state ('first fruits', v.20). Finally, adopting a different perspective, Paul can detach Christ somewhat from those who are connected to him, seeing him as the 'head' of 'every man' (I Cor. 11.3), meaning probably (in view of the allusion to Eve's formation from Adam in Gen. 2) 'origin', and surely assuming the sense of 'every *Christian* man'. This detaching of Christ as 'head', or rather relaxing the sense of identification implicit in Paul's 'in Christ' language and in his use of the image of the 'body' in I Cor.12, was developed in Colossians and Ephesians, stressing Christ's universal and heavenly lordship over the dependent church (see Martin Kitchen, *Ephesians*).

After all the fluidity in I Corinthians, Paul did nevertheless return to a version of the concept in I Cor. 12 when he came to write Romans. In ch. 12, having given his long sketch of God's grand design for Jews and gentiles to attain their due consummation in a visionary future, Paul steps back, and picks up the ethical thread with which the opening chapters of Romans were in part concerned. In that context the collaborative image of the body serves once more to counter tendencies to ego-inflation, this time not so much on the basis of exciting spiritual gifts as in relation to general moral attitudes. Moreover, the image itself is not exploited with the same christological intensity. Instead of the direct and strong, 'You are the body of Christ and individually members of it', which forms the punchy climax of Paul's rather laboured exposition of the theme in I Cor. 12 (v. 27, cf. the equally strong v.12 which opens the passage), we have the following: 'we, though many, are one body in Christ and individually members one of another'. Here there is not the same close identification of 'the body' with Christ himself: it is more of an illustration, an aid to moral instruction and a means of urging mutual moral responsibility. This should not surprise us: in Rom. 9–11 his whole orientation has been not so much christological as salvation-historical, and the community's place in the historical continuum has been chiefly in mind; by contrast with the Christ-centred new-ness of the church which is Paul's dominant picture in I Corinthians.

3

The Church and the Gospels

I have already referred to some of the difficulties that present themselves when one turns to the Gospels in search of early Christian ways of thinking about their community and its place as a phenomenon in the world. It is time to focus on those problems more closely.

On a straightforward reading, of course, the Gospels have very little bearing on our subject. They tell the story of Jesus and are mostly concerned with his acts and his teaching. They show little sign that Jesus preoccupied himself with organizational matters, whether involving ideas comparable to those so striking in Paul or not. In so far as a picture of a community of Jesus' followers appears, it is chiefly in the defined but otherwise informal group of the Twelve, and apart from such 'tribes of Israel' echoes as are implicit in their very existence (and no statement draws attention to this apart from the future hope in Matt. 19.28 and Luke 22.30), nothing is said to encourage any tendency to theorize about them. Leaving aside the texts just mentioned (which concern rule at the End – puzzlingly, unless the one is a figure for the other, over not the church but the tribes of Israel), we are told that the task of the Twelve is mission on behalf of the kingdom (Mark 6.1–6; Matt. 10; Luke 9 and 10), described largely in terms which make them reproduce the activity and proclamation of Jesus himself; and, after his life-time, for

Matthew, the propagation of Jesus' whole teaching (28.16–20). Otherwise, we can only point to the two uses of the word *ekklesia* in Matthew (16.19; 18.17), which even a hypothetical straightforward reader might suspect of being the product of post-Jesus developments. If they were authentic, they would of course testify to Jesus as envisioning both the church as an institution (16.19) and the church as localized group (18.17), that is, both the senses found in the letters of Paul. That might seem improbable, especially in the absence from the Gospels of communities to which the term seems applicable.

If these two uses of *ekklesia* in fact raise in a striking way the question of reference in the Gospels to circumstances after the life-time of Jesus, they prompt us to take this approach to the Gospels in general. However difficult it may be to be sure of results where the evidence is so inexplicit (the Gospels are indeed set in the past of Jesus' life-time), it is necessary to explore the possibility that they also throw light on the circumstances of their writing, even if in less obvious ways than the Matthean example quoted above. This would include the way the Christian communities responsible for producing and receiving the Gospels thought of themselves in the light of their beliefs concerning Jesus and their devotion to him. Obviously the quest is tentative in a way that was not true of the investigation of Paul's ideas on this subject. It is worth noting that any such heading as 'Mark's ecclesiology' would hardly have been suggested until recent years, and remains more elusive than, say, Mark's christology or eschatology. Yet the possibility has long been in the wings: ever since form critics saw the Gospel sections as developing in church use in the years before the writing down, it has been possible to see the church as showing through in the episodes of the narrative themselves.

Two strategies offer themselves: first, viewing the narrative as such through ecclesiological eyes; that is, if we think in 'church' terms, how does Mark read? Can this story be read fruitfully in a churchly perspective? And second, if we envisage the live context in which such a book as this was written, what picture of itself would the community have held? In other words, we may adopt either a more literary or a more historical point of departure. We can have both strategies in mind as we read the Gospels.

In this enquiry, the disciples as a group are the obvious prime candidates for consideration. Once we think about the Gospels in this way, we can see that, whether it was done deliberately or not, it would be almost inevitable for the disciples to reflect in some measure the church as known to the evangelist. This might not, however, be free of ambiguity. Thus: do they reflect the church as the evangelist experiences it, or the church as he would like it to be, or the church as he believes it was in the days of Jesus? In other words, is it a realistic or idealized church that is reflected? Further: the disciples may indeed reflect the church as a whole, but they may (also or instead, sometimes or all through) rather reflect Christian leaders. What is more, inchoate as they are, 'the crowds' are also possible representations of the church. In the stories of the feedings, for example, it is not difficult to see these two last possibilities combined: the disciples as 'ministers' handing food to the 'lay' congregation in a quasi-eucharist. How early in Christian reflection would such an understanding (and telling) of the story be plausible? With these uncertain possibilities in mind, we consider the Gospels in turn, for each has its own character, in this as in all matters.

The Gospel of Mark

The first chapter of the Gospel of Mark already illustrates the difficulties of this kind of doctrinal enquiry where a narrative such as a Gospel is concerned. It is now customary – and no doubt helpful – to think in terms of the opening sections of Mark as a prologue, comparable to that of the Gospel of John. By 'prologue', we presumably mean a statement that both introduces the work as a whole and stands apart from the rest of the narrative in stating themes and ideas which are normative for the whole book – rather like the overture at certain stages in the history of opera. In our present terms, it sets out the author's theological stall in at least some of its essentials. Now, in that light, what is the extent of Mark's prologue? Modern editions often view Mark in this way and state an opinion by placing a gap at a particular point, usually after 1.11 or 1.13. There is a case to be made for either of those decisions, and in both it means in effect taking the position that Mark's normative, 'prologuish' statement is christological in purpose: what the reader needs to grasp as key to the whole, in Mark's view, is the identity of Jesus as the agent of God's purpose. It will be much the same if vv. 14–15 are counted within the prologue, though now the accent will fall rather more on Jesus' message as essential to the normative doctrinal statement. These verses after all have so much the character of a summary of that message that they qualify very well to be included in a preliminary statement of the Gospel's purpose. But what of 1.16–20? It is an intermediate passage, describing the call of four disciples, before Mark embarks on a series of healings and other episodes that reads like a set of sample items in Jesus' ministry. The twin calls in these verses are described – like the preaching in vv. 14–15 – with utmost brevity:

Jesus' summons elicits the instant response of following, joining Jesus for whatever he does and stands for. The fact that the four are not mentioned in many of the subsequent episodes (only once as a complete group, 13.3) only serves to point up the representative character of this section. It too may then sensibly be seen as belonging to and concluding the prologue in Mark's design. If so, it means that Mark views the community round Jesus as part and parcel of the essence of his story. In formal terms, ecclesiology belongs with christology in the Christian message, flows from it and is inseparable from it. We may say that, seen in this light, Mark promises to give us a catholic rather than a protestant book! There is, in the essence of Christianity, church as well as message; or the church is integral to the message. But does the rest of Mark bear out such a reading? Does his narrative as a whole have a notable ecclesiological dimension?

Once this perspective is adopted, even only as a working hypothesis, then, allowing for the ambiguity between disciples and crowd as bearers of the church's identity (an ambiguity perhaps not only in the text as text but also unresolved in Mark's own mind), it casts its light over the whole book and opens up a way of reading many of its episodes.

The overwhelming impression is that, despite the absence of Paul's images and terms ('in Christ', 'body of Christ') that express the intimacy of Jesus with the community and the latter's dependence on him for meaning and for resources, this is here too the nature of the relationship between Jesus and his disciples. The commonest word for that relationship is 'follow', used eighteen times, sometimes (e.g. 2.14–15) in clusters so that it would impress itself on the hearers when the book was read aloud (as always for many years). Sometimes a theological resonance is unlikely (e.g. 14.13) or uncertain, but there can be a poignant irony in Peter's following 'from afar' after Jesus' arrest (14.54), so different from the willing following in 1.18. In Mark's perception, a 'disciple' is not chiefly a pupil or apprentice (the core sense of *mathetes*) but a follower. So much is this the case that though the disciples can be sent out on mission and instructed for the task, separation from Jesus (even by his being asleep) is regularly depicted as leading to failure (4.35–41; 6.45–52; 9.14–29; 14.37).

'Follow' conveys attachment to Jesus which can in theory be an individual affair; but Mark's most typical model for the community is that of surrogate family. It is implicit in 1.20, almost brutally stated in 3.21, 31–35 (with 6.1–6), and laid out formally in 10.28–31. To become a follower of Jesus is to enter a new household, however restless or itinerant the Jesus community might in practice be. It involves renunciation of former links and exclusive loyalty to those now taken on. It is abandonment that carries the assurance of gain and is the absolute condition of that gain (8.35). The new household is moreover one of equality and simplicity (10.13–16, 35–45). Mark gives no honours or preference to leaders and brushes the notion aside: that is a major step in the prevailing culture, where honour and precision in the recognition of status were matters of acute sensitivity. Further, the policy of equality embraces gentiles alongside Jews (7.24–30; 11.17; 15.39). It is hard to see how the hearer of Mark could avoid identifying these characteristics as the primary aspirations or features of the Christian community – for which, interestingly, this Gospel gives no hint of a name: we have no idea how Mark's community would have described itself, unless it was as 'the followers'.

The only relationship exempt from this family-replacement is marriage: note the omission of 'wife' and 'husband' from the lists in 10.29 and 31. This exception is positively strengthened in the explanation a little earlier of why divorce is now ruled out (10.1–12): for the followers of Jesus, the conditions of Eden are now restored (just as for Paul they experience a new creation under the lordship of a new Adam). It may be that this material has in mind not marriage disruptions in general but specifically those occasioned by one party's Christian allegiance. Paul considered such situations and was indulgent (I Cor. 7.10–15). Mark's Jesus is much less so, but provides an ideal (is it exactly a law, as Matthew's parallel provision, 19.1–9, more clearly is?) in relation to marriage that is to be cherished.

That Christian allegiance is a threat to existing family relationships is confirmed in ch.13, the apocalypse (vv. 12–13). When the Gospel involves crisis, as it will supremely when the Son of man returns and the kingdom comes in power (13.26; 9.1), families will split. The responsibility for the rupture, now and in the future, rests with those who refuse Jesus' call. This clear treatment of the theme in the important context of ch. 13 doubtless indicates where the weight fell for Mark: it is both the call of Jesus in his life-time, renewed through the hearing of Mark's words, and the future consummation, which set the scene for the formation and self-understanding of the church as the community of the saved. And this prospect of crisis, for both natural and ecclesial families, is presented, with typical apocalyptic hyperbole, against a backcloth of cosmic disaster (13.5–11). Such is the not inconsiderable importance that Mark attributes to the community whose representative he is in the writing of his Gospel.

It is often suggested that the distinctiveness and

separateness of the community – surely in a setting of physical proximity to the rest of society – are symbolized in the thrice-used image of the boat (4.35–41; 6.45–52; 8.13–21), where the disciples are isolated with Jesus (in the second case, precariously so). Given the link with bread-sharing in most of these passages, the upper room of the final supper serves the same end: the enclosure where the holy ones, imperfect as they so clearly are in Mark, meet with Jesus.

For our purpose – that of identifying Mark's doctrine of the church – it is not necessary to speculate further about the setting or social make-up of this community (see H.C. Kee, *Community of the New Age*), or to decide whether Mark's emphasis on features such as simplicity, abandon-ment and the necessity of suffering points to their reluc-tance to embrace these very things. Nor is it necessary to attend to the historical problems raised by Mark's less than enthusiastic depiction of the disciples (6.52; 8.21; 14.32–50): they are well described as 'flawed followers', both words deserving emphasis; though this candid presentation, whatever its explanation, does at least indi-cate that Mark resists any tendency to idealize the church or to make of its first manifestation (and, in some cases at least, early leaders) a community of heroes. If Mark finds heroes, it is in individuals who respond to Jesus or to God with open willingness: 10.52; 12.41–44; 14.3–9; though this purity of action is not ruled out as a characteristic of the 'official' disciples – at least in their paradigm moment, 1.16–20, and in the supreme insight offered to them (9.2; 16.5–6).

How far Mark looks beyond his own local group and pictures terms of membership that apply to all Jesus' followers, we have no way of knowing; though what we see of the effectiveness of 'net-working' in the first-century church (e.g. from Paul's letters), and what we know of the speedy spread of this Gospel beyond its place of origin (it was soon used by Matthew and Luke), point to wider horizons being available, perhaps inevitable. It would be surprising too if the author was entirely home-grown as a Christian, without substantial debts to others before him in other localities, other Christian communities.

The Gospel of Matthew

Mark's practical attention centres on the substitution of one household for another, such a move in his society (as in many others) signifying in large measure the substitution of one whole identity for another. Matthew shares this awareness, reproducing the passages chiefly concerned, but he puts them in sharper focus. It seems that his institutional awareness is more acute, his sensitivity to institutional needs and realities more explicit. What is involved here is not just the arrival of a new community, initiated by Jesus, with certain profound and demanding characteristics (like abandonment of former ties and a sense of close internal cohesion), but a body of adherents of Jesus who have tasks to perform and problems to face, as the very stuff of their communal life. With this goes a stronger feeling for their own distinctiveness: they are more aware that they are not as others are. Perhaps surprisingly, given the force of images of segregation, like the boat at sea, Mark had still been keen to recruit all possible help in the cause of the kingdom and to turn away none who were well-disposed ('the one who is not against us is on our side', 9.40). It is a doctrine that Matthew simply reverses: 'the one who is not with me is against me' (12.30). There could be no sharper testimony to the shift in awareness. Developed and formalized, it would even amount to a contradiction in ecclesiology, and much in the history of Christian thought in this area could be expounded in terms of the contrast.

The evidence of the shift is mostly less dramatic, though visible nevertheless. It comes mostly in the form of additions to Mark's stories or amendments to their wording. In the former category, there is the explicit reference to the Christian community as a separate entity from the Jewish people who were, in Matthew's eyes, responsible (as a whole, 27.25) for the rejection and execution of Jesus, the plainly accredited Messiah (e.g. 1–2; 21.5): 21.42–43 – 'the kingdom of God will be taken away from you'. This communal displacement of the Jews was perhaps implicit in Mark, but it did not quite achieve formal expression: the attention was elsewhere – so much on the wonder of the new allegiance that communal and institutional implications were largely ignored. Similarly, the encomium on Peter (16.17–19) serves not only to free him from the ignominy in which Mark's swift exchange leaves him (8.27–33) and so to legitimate his stature and leadership in the church, but also to license the church (*ekklesia*) itself, apparently as a whole institution, wherever it might be found; and the universal commission in 28.16–20 shows that the vision had no bounds. It was as unlimited as the sovereignty of Christ himself.

Among the amendments to Mark's wording, there is the stricter description of the 'family' of Jesus: no longer the rather amorphous group of 'those around him' (Mark 3.35), but the defined and known body of 'his disciples', gathered under Jesus' hand of blessing (12.46–50). There is also the somewhat more formalized setting out of the call of the first disciples (4.18–22), with the reiteration of 'brother', which in the light of 23.8 (and 12.50) appears as a normative description of church members: they are a band of brothers (with sisters scarcely figuring – just 27.55, taken from Mark).

The same tendency is to be seen in Matthew's enhanced sense of differentiation among 'the disciples' – the greater singling out of Peter (4.18; 14.31–33; 16.17–19) and the giving to them of authority in the congregation (18.18) and of formal judicial powers over 'the twelve tribes of Israel' (19.28) as auxiliaries to the triumphant Jesus, with its possible significance for the character and place of structures in Matthew's concept of the church. But it is evident that, even leaving aside patterns of leadership, Matthew has a strong sense of the detailed life of the Christian community and its needs. Thus, in Jesus' five discourses, it is provided with wide-ranging and balanced guidance for all sides of its existence and work, as if Matthew had presented himself (or been presented) with a considered agenda and the following topics were to be covered: basic moral orientation (5–7), mission (10), congregational regulation (18), ultimate expectations (24–25). The middle discourse, consisting of parables, ch. 13, an extension of Mark's material in ch. 4, is in effect an expansion and underlining in parable form of points made in ch. 10 on missionary work (sower, pearl and treasure) and in ch. 18 on church regulation (tares and dragnet). All may be said to relate, using Matthew's typical terminology, to various aspects of the kingdom of heaven, in present and future, all seen in a church perspective. In the light of Matthew's practical bent, we should perhaps take it that his Christian community, in actuality or in design, has both itinerant (10) and sedentary (18) 'departments' of activity. Both modes are approved, encouraged and provided for. As the Didache was to show, it would not always be so and itinerants would become objects of suspicion in some of the settled Christian communities.

Indeed, it may already have been the case that some of Paul's troubles (e.g. at Corinth) stemmed from internal congregational irritation with Paul, the apostle who, if not itinerant in the sense depicted in the Gospels for Jesus in Galilee and (we suggest) for some of Matthew's Christians, was an absentee from their everyday church life, who nevertheless claimed the right to supervise and intervene from afar and from time to time. Matthew's overarching strategy and church-consciousness were such as to embrace both sides of that only too understandable picture, with its rich potential for conflict.

The mainly new, non-Markan material in ch. 18, about disciplinary questions within the congregation (with *ekklesia* now appearing in this local sense, v.17), illustrates very well Matthew's intensified feeling for the community as institution. (In relation to Mark, it is a development akin to that in some of the writings in the Pauline tradition, such as Ephesians and the Pastorals, that bear Paul's name.) But perhaps Matthew's most striking move was to transfer Marcan teaching about trials and feuds to be expected by the Christian community in the coming eschatological crisis (Mark 13.9–13) to the instructions for missionaries (Matt. 10.17–22). In other words, such trials and tribulations, attacks and disputes with relations, are now part and parcel of the daily life of missionaries of the kingdom, daily expectations for followers of Jesus in their strenuous work.

It is wholly in line with Matthew's more defined ecclesial sense that in this Gospel 'kingdom of heaven' (or 'of God') begins to acquire overtones of 'the church', a doctrinal move with a powerful future in store for it. Still, as in Mark, chiefly eschatological, it is already experienced in Jesus' presence (12.28) and so, by implication and extension, in his community. In 18.23–35, 'the kingdom' is compared to a situation where forgiveness is required and failure to forgive brings condemnation. But precisely this process has just been outlined for life in the congregation, with Jesus invisibly present to ratify judgments made by his followers (18.15–20). References to the kingdom in passages like 13.44, 45 also carry application to the life and work of the church here and now. In effect Matthew seems to affirm a seamless continuity between Christ's community in the present and the great consummation for which its members are warned (on pain of dire punishment) to be always vigilant. Jesus himself is equally present in both phases: 18.20; 28.20; cf. 13.41; 25.31–46. This central fact was implicit in his birth-name, Emmanuel, 'God-with-us' (1.23).

In strict first-century terms and in the light of Paul's anguish of identity in relation to Judaism, the most important element in all this is the separateness of the church, which Matthew seems to be not just accepting but asserting, not only in the added statements in 21.42f. about the failure of Israel and the church's inheriting of its God-given role, but also in the repeated, distancing references to '*their* synagogues' (by contrast, it seems, to '*our* church', 4.23; 9.35; 12.9; 13.54). Here again institutional awareness, conveyed in a favourite yet almost unconscious phrase, is to the fore. Yet this is no cutting away from roots. The new community is the proper heir of all the property of the old, summarized as 'law and prophets'. It is its refurbisher and proud user: 5.17–48; 22.40; 23.3, 33. But all this it lives out as the people of the Messiah, secure in his company (28.20) and under his guardianship (11.28–30). Matthew thus has the best of both his worlds: he has a well-thought-out idea of age-old scriptural roots and of a firmly based inheritance, together with a full conviction of the splendour of God's new and definitive gift in Jesus.

The Gospel of Luke and the Acts of the Apostles

As far as the Gospel of Luke is concerned, the same set of problems arises as we found in interpreting Mark and Matthew, and solutions put forward are in a single spectrum with those reached in the two earlier cases. Most obviously, there is the question how far (if indeed at all) the Gospel reflects, in its depiction of the life of Jesus, perspectives and beliefs that belong to the subsequent period, and in particular those of the author and of the Christians around him. Further, if this is the case, the Gospel may reflect the beliefs of the author's own time only in an indirect sense: that is, he may depict the time of Jesus in the light not so much of the realities of his own day as of his own ideals for his own situation: what he wishes the church were like may be expressed in the context given to Jesus' person, teaching and activity. In other words, there is a hortatory element, perhaps dominantly so, in the presentation, addressed to the evangelist's own generation. In that case, the beliefs implicit in Luke's telling of the story, whether they concern the Christian community or other matters, would reflect neither those of Jesus and his immediate followers precisely nor those of Luke's community, but rather those that he wished were more evident in their self-understanding and in their common life. Several important aspects of Luke's depiction have, with plausibility (especially where they differ from the other Gospels), come to be presented in this light.

In the case of Luke, the situation is further complicated by his having carried the story forward into his second volume, the Acts of the Apostles. This is not the place to go into the matter, but there is strong indication that this is not a case of two independently planned books, each presenting its own allotted narrative, but of a single largely unitary conception, one grand design. Quite apart from links at the level of parallel items in stories (e.g. Luke 23.34, 46 and Acts 7.60, 59), there are numerous common emphases, some of which affect closely the author's beliefs about the church.

In Acts, once more, the question of aspiration versus description arises. For some crucial matters, however, a test can be applied. The letters of Paul, already perhaps thirty years old by the time of Acts, offer both a check and, more importantly, a point of comparison when it comes to making a correct reading of Acts; for the two sources overlap in their coverage of certain events. The letters furnish us with two distinct aids in this respect. First, they give us a sense of church life which is in several ways at variance with the picture in Acts; and second, their ways of expressing beliefs about Christian community are different from those of Acts. We consider these two matters in turn.

First, the two pictures of church life. In the letters we find a tragic contrast between Paul's sense of the church as a community integrally united with Christ and at peace in itself, with all its constituent parts functioning in harmony, and the realities with which he had to contend – both in internal congregational life, as at Corinth, and in the very heart of the church's mission and self-understanding, as in his failure to reach a lasting and wholehearted agreement with the Jewish-Christian establishment on such basic matters as the acceptance of gentiles. In Acts, on the other hand, there is a sense of an essentially unimpeded and unstoppable onward march of the gospel, with disagreements soon settled and passing antagonisms only releasing fresh energy for the future (as in the dispute in ch. 6 between Aramaic and Greek-speaking Jewish Christians in Jerusalem, the council in ch. 15, and the tiff over Mark in 15.35ff.). Even if Acts is partly motivated by the desire to keep Christian spirits up by an appeal to the great days of the church's beginnings, serious ecclesiology is implicit in its telling of the story; for this author, the church is cohesive in practice as well as in conviction and aspiration, and its mission almost has a charmed life, as it overcomes all obstacles and survives all trials and afflictions from whatever quarter they come. The up-beat conclusion of the book, with Paul at work in Rome 'unhindered', defies even the might of Rome and will not let us see, let alone dwell on, his ensuing martyrdom. (The frank recognition of Luke's theologico-ideological motivation, notably in his picture of Paul's story, was first strikingly advanced by John Knox, *Chapters in a Life of Paul*. See also, more recently, Gerd Lüdemann, *Paul, Apostle to the Gentiles*.)

There is a comparable contrast with regard to the related matter of Jew-gentile relations in the church. In Paul's genuine letters (contrast Eph. 2.11–22) this issue remains live and bitterly controverted to the end of Paul's observable career. Despite agreement about spheres of missionary activity (Gal. 2.1–10), perceptions of what this involves for relations within the Christian community remain wide apart: witness the collapse of fellowship in Antioch (Gal. 2.11ff.) and the subsequent subversion of Paul's mission in church after church, as II Corinthians, Galatians and Philippians show. Paul's ready acceptance of gentiles on the basis of faith in Christ alone, and so, from a Jewish-Christian point of view, on falsely liberal terms, remained unacceptable. In Acts, however, there is an early resolution of the difficulty, arrived at in a wholly eirenical, positive and forward-looking way (Acts 15), and on this basis Paul is free to continue his mission in security as far as church backing is concerned. And on his final visit to the Jerusalem church (Acts 21), though he encounters opposition from the populace that opens the

way to his arrest and trials, he meets nothing but thankful
approbation from the leaders of the church (21.20); as for
Jewish converts there who have not yet seen the light, a
devout, Torah gesture should suffice to win them over
(21.21–24). The Paul of Acts (but the Paul of history?)
willingly conforms in the interests of harmony. What is
more, Luke had adumbrated just such an outcome: in 3.6,
he firmly rounds off the quotation from Isa. 40, 'and all
flesh shall see the salvation of God'; and Jesus had
flamboyantly endorsed God's open favour to gentiles,
4.24–29. Acts throughout sees the Jew-gentile issue as
rightly and effectively susceptible of solution by compromise, rather than stark choice (Acts 15.20, an agreement
whose terms are themselves almost certainly seen as scripturally provided). How far this is a result of a historical
perspective that includes Israel's whole history as provi-
dentially ordered and how far it derives rather from a
practical desire on the part of Luke to give both Jews and
gentiles an accepted and settled place in the church, both
letting bygones be bygones, it is hard to know. At all
events, he shows a keen desire that this problem should
now be put behind Christians – as new forces of division
begin to show themselves (Acts 20.29–31). Whatever
their precise character, these threats lend urgency to the
emphasis on the past achievement of harmony: it is a
legacy not to be squandered.

This leads naturally to the second matter I referred to:
Paul and the author of Luke-Acts have different modes,
not just of telling the story, but also of expressing beliefs
about the Christian community. Where Paul works with
symbols (body, bride, etc.), and even in his historical argu-
mentation makes much of symbolic figures like Adam and
Abraham, Luke-Acts presents us with a community that
has an identifiable, describable continuity in scriptural

history. Of course Jesus is the crucial turning-point in that process, but process it is nevertheless. It is natural that *ekklesia* can refer to Israel in the wilderness (Acts 7.38), and then to Christian congregations (18 times) – but then, we saw it is used appropriately and naturally for the civic assembly in Acts 19, so it may not be reflected on theologically very much at all; and the fact that, with the exception perhaps of 9.31 and 20.28, the term never denotes anything wider than a congregation makes it hard to feel that, at any rate by way of this word, this author works with much of a picture, still less a concept, of the Christian people as a whole. Certainly, in never using it in the Gospel, he gives no ground (again, by way of this word) for seeing Jesus-plus-disciples as a paradigm of the Christian community of later times. It may be that, for Luke, the resonances of the word are not theologically rich, and he will use other methods.

More interestingly, at first sight Luke has no sense that the church is to be thought of christologically, that is, integrated conceptually with Jesus, as the great Pauline images insist so forcefully. In Acts, there is heavenly guidance and inspiration but no language to suggest anything like the almost fused identity we find in Paul. What we do have, however, in the Gospel, is a picture of beneficent and sympathetic companionship between Jesus and his disciples; the question is how to evaluate that picture. Nowhere is it more striking than in the passion story, where Mark's feeble disciples are virtually excused for their behaviour – the Gethsemene sleepers for their understandable fatigue (22.45), Peter for having natural fear exploited by the devil and in any case only briefly (22.31f.), and even Judas who is also seen as a victim of diabolic seizure (22.3). It is also the case that episodes in Mark and Matthew that reflect badly on the disciples simply do not appear; for example, the request for chief places in the kingdom (Mark 10.35–45); and when part of this material finds a place at the table of the last supper (22.24–27), the tone is of gentle fraternal instruction rather than rebuke. Neither of two Marcan 'boat' stories that display the disciples' blundering incomprehension finds a place in Luke's narrative (Mark 6.45–52; 8.14–21). At a more sober level, this theme of companionship is transmuted in Acts, as Jesus' followers are shown enduring sufferings in a spirit akin to that of Jesus himself, and indeed with events themselves half-reminding us of the passion of Jesus: most obviously in the case of Stephen (see especially Acts 6.13; 7.59–60), but also perhaps in the case of Peter in Acts 12 and even Paul's shipwreck in Acts 27, with its quasi-eucharistic feeding in v.35f. and its sugges-tive use of *soteria* in v.34 ('this is for your salvation/strength').

If this picture of beneficent and faithful companionship (in life and in suffering) tells us anything about Luke's idea of the church as well as about his understanding of how things must have been in Jesus' life-time and in the years immediately following, then it certainly speaks for what we might describe as an ecclesiology of memory as a primary element in the church's self-awareness: we are the community that we are because of this impulse, this model. It would then be paralleled in the portrayal of the (idealized?) Jerusalem church in Acts 1–4, with its equally beneficent and loving life-style.

The main difficulty with this reading of the Gospel's treatment of Jesus' disciples as a prototype and exemplar of the church is that, much more than in Mark and even more than in Matthew, there is a strong case for the view that Luke sees 'the apostles' (his favoured term) as church leaders rather than rank and file: the use of the word in the

Gospel (six times) may point to the distinction being thrown back from Acts, where it is plain in the picture of the church in Jerusalem as made up of both leaders and led. But perhaps it is not necessary to choose between these two roles for the Lucan disciples. Proto-leaders they may be – and this may help to account for Luke's reluctance to say anything to their discredit – but they are also proto-church: the distinction between leaders and led does not extend to ideals of ethical life or relation to Jesus. The disciples receive both as Jesus' gifts in the Gospel.

Luke's firmly narrative mode precludes the use of strongly conceptual language, but, contrary to initial appearances, it may be right to conclude that Luke does after all have an implicit doctrine of the church that is rooted in christology: in the sense that to be 'church' is to be in Jesus' circle, nowhere more typically than at table receiving his friendship and teaching. So far, Luke and John share an idea of the church as fellowship with Jesus, impregnated with his life. Both have paradigmatic supper discourses (Luke 22.14–38; John 14–17). Yet, if the church is for Luke to be seen, simply but powerfully, as 'the companions of Jesus', it is not wholly comparable to, for example, the group of pupils that surrounds a teacher; despite the fact that Luke's frequent portrayal of Jesus teaching at table (5.29–32; 11.37–52; 14.1–24; 22.14–38) has indeed been taken to be modelled on the literary convention of the symposium where a philosopher discourses with his disciples who are also his friends. There may be an element of truth in this suggestion, but there is a ferocity of criticism in some of Jesus' speeches at meals that scarcely coheres with the cool quest for abstract truth. He is not always among friends, but often among potential enemies.

There is moreover another dimension to Luke's beliefs

about Jesus and it points in a different (though possibly not incompatible) direction. We have seen that Luke is deeply concerned to give equal recognition to both Jews and gentiles in the church and to promote unity between them. In connection with this concern and in part in its furtherance, Luke is at pains to demonstrate Jesus' pedigree in scriptural history, seen as traceable not merely to Abraham (see Matt. 1.1–17) but to Adam, initiator of the human race (3.38). Yet this physical inheritance, seen as fortified by prophecy (24.26, 43f.), is put alongside Jesus' emergence from a sacred Jewish setting redolent of old scriptural piety (Luke 1.5–2.52). Jesus is no deracinated manifestation of divine intentions, and the church, stemming from him and succeeding to him, is no novelty but the inheritor of Israel itself. Its origins in Jerusalem (Acts 1–8; 15; 21) make the point clear. Luke abstains from describing the events of 70CE that would be ruinous to his eirenic purpose and his sense of harmonious development, though he foreshadows them in Luke 19.41–44 and elsewhere and can see them only as inevitable tragedy. They do not however affect Luke's overarching picture of God's salvific history. Jesus as the fulfiller of Israel-provided hopes and roles signifies that the torch is not extinguished but survives and flourishes in the hands of his followers, spread world-wide.

It is likely that Luke was particularly concerned, alongside his purpose of mission to all, to safeguard precisely this perception of the church as the heir of the Jewish past. We cannot be sure, but it is not unlikely that he was faced not only with the task of welding Jewish and gentile Christians into a single community, but also with incipient discontent from increasingly dominant gentile Christians impatient with the legacy of Jewishness – in scriptures, religious terms and customs, and reverence for the setting into which Jesus came. Even in the modified form in which some of these elements survived in Luke's picture of correct church policy (Acts 15.20 was surely his guide, the symbol of his symbiotic ideal), there must have been a questioning of their continuing relevance, and perhaps an awareness that other Christian groups, also admirers of Paul, adopted a more radical approach. This is speculative, but what cannot be denied is that Luke goes to great lengths to foster affirmation of, and even affection for, that Jewish inheritance.

The Jerusalem council, where Paul, having conducted his first, 'pilot' mission, meets with the Jerusalem leaders (Acts 15), is pivotal to the whole story told in Acts, perhaps in that from Luke 1 to Acts 28, both theologically and in terms of narrative. The preceding phases of development, not just in Acts but in the Gospel too, lead up to this climax, especially if we look at the whole story from an ecclesial standpoint; and, in the sweep of the narrative, the success of Paul's wide mission in Greek cities and, ultimately, in Rome flows directly from the impulse the council gives and the opening it affords for wide-ranging mission in gentile lands. That council establishes the church firmly as a joint Jew-gentile enterprise and offers no scope for any other conception of its identity. For all the imposition of compromise conditions on gentile converts (15.20), so inimical to Paul's conduct in his lifetime as expressed in his letters, their theological significance and objective is the same as Paul's: unity and harmony between the two elements in the one church; only now, in the years after 70CE when Luke is writing, the threat may be coming not any longer from Jewish Christians in positions of authority but (as suggested above) from gentile Christians impatient with the Jewish 'luggage' attaching to the gospel. In the post-70 situation, it was probably even harder to hold a church together than it was to preserve the morale of Jewish communities: a church had so much less to draw on as tangible marks of identity, and with the Jerusalem headquarters gone, it must have seemed vital to hold on to possessions like the old scriptures, in order to avoid dissolution into a rather shapeless and rootless Jesus-piety. It is against this background that we should view Luke's picture of the ideal Christian community (Acts 1.15; 9.30; 10.23; 11.1,29) of the first days in Jerusalem and its structured common life (2.42–44), living under the strong power of the Spirit (2.1–4) and marvellous in its success (2.41; 4–5; 6.7; 21.20).

The Gospel of John

There is a serious question whether the Fourth Gospel contains a doctrine of the church. No one would suggest that its author was a lone Christian, pursuing his faith in isolation and unconnected with other Christians; but it is possible to be related to a group without having thought-out beliefs about it or ideas about its place in your total scheme of things. The proposal would be that this writer sees Jesus as attracting to himself a series of individuals whose spiritual and theological eye is on him alone as the source or intermediary of salvation. In support of such a view, it is possible to point to a succession of episodes which consist of an extended dialogue between Jesus and an individual, or in relation to an individual: the Samaritan woman in ch.4, the paralytic in ch.5, and the man born blind in ch.9; possible also to interpret the apparently corporate images of the flock in ch.10 and the vine in ch.15 in individualistic terms – each sheep is called in its own right ('by name') and each branch is separately joined to the vine. This view is, however, certainly not mandatory and is likely to come to the fore chiefly where the Gospel is understood as incipiently gnostic in outlook and provenance. It is true that, like the other Gospels apart from Matthew, John never uses the word *ekklesia* or any synonym (though it appears in III John); but, as we have seen, the mere absence of the word by no means precludes the presence of a developed sense of the Christian community and its theological significance, or indeed of means whereby ideas about it are expressed. Like the other Gospels, John in fact offers ample evidence of a well-articulated doctrine of the church, and its essential lines are much the same as those we have found, though with divergence of mode, in those writings and indeed in Paul.

Above all, belief about the church functions in harmony with and is wholly dependent on belief about Jesus. Ecclesiology is an offshoot of christology, and in no sense an independent subject able to sprout its own agenda or operate under its own rules. Yet it would be wrong to see ecclesiology as merely an afterthought, a by-product of more fundamental concerns. Rather, it is integral to John's picture and message that Jesus, sent by the Father, calls people to himself and forms them into a community that is one with him as he is one with the Father (10.30; 17.11). It is not possible to argue that this framework is envisaged only for the life-time of Jesus – quite the contrary: in outlining its terms, Jesus looks on to those who believe in him through the word of the initial circle of adherents (17.20–23). So organic continuity is established, a succession of persons who are the objects of Jesus' love as he is the object of the Father's love, and who indeed, in 20.29, receive the greater blessing of those 'who have not seen and yet believe'. And even this does not exhaust the scope of this community. Much of John's presentation does indeed indicate a closed group, gathered out of 'the world' that is seen as hostile (15.18f; 17.14); and the whole scene-setting of the supper-room for chs 13–17, the great discourse formative of the church, indicates withdrawal from the world at large that is the setting for the first half of the Gospel, with a sense of separation, mutual exclusion and privileged access to the Father through Jesus. Yet that is not the whole of the story: witness to the world and hope for its salvation remain. It is after all God's creation through the Word (1.1–3) and the object of his love (3.16). That 'the world may believe that thou didst send me' is the stated purpose of the formation of the community of Jesus' followers (17.21).

This vision beyond the enclosure of the church is already established (like all the main strands of the Johannine vision) in the prologue (1.1–18). The light lightens everyone (1.9); and while the 'we' who have beheld the glory of the Word-made-flesh no doubt signifies primarily those who have received him (1.12–14), the pronoun gains a shadow of broader meaning from the perspective in v.9. And the world as the object of God's love is the basis for Jesus' whole mission (3.16).

A number of verbal features fortify an ecclesial understanding of this Gospel. Most obvious of all is the frequency of reference to 'the disciples' (greater than in any of the other Gospels): as we have just seen, they signify (and must surely from the start have been heard or read as signifiying) more than simply the band of Jesus' original followers and associates. They are the Gospel's audience as well as among its *dramatis personae*. They appear in every major episode of Jesus' ministry (except ch. 5).

The Spirit-Paraclete in chs 14–16 is from one angle the binding force, almost the personification (see 'he will

witness . . . you also witness', 15.26f.) of the church – the
clear sign, if one were still needed, that John thinks in
terms of a solidarity, not an assemblage of individuals. The
Spirit is also rightly seen as Jesus' *alter ego* (14.16,18). So
the Spirit is the common factor between the time of Jesus
and the time of the church: 1.33 and 20.22. As the Spirit is
a leading term for expressing Jesus' divine empowerment,
so it remains in the same role for the church. Thereby it
reduces the gap between Jesus and the church, stabilizing
the church as the inheritor and perpetuator of what Jesus
represented. So the Spirit will take the things of Jesus and
'declare them to you' (16.14f.). Some modern critics have
been inclined to see this Gospel as more removed from the
words of the historical Jesus than any other and as having
something of the character of a free meditation on his
person and teaching. The writer himself would not have
understood that view, whatever was the method of its
composition and use of sources. He doubtless saw himself
as an agent of the Spirit, bringing forth clearly and faith-
fully 'the things of Jesus'; just as the Spirit also defends the
church when it is subjected to challenge and accusation
(16.8–11). Which of the followers of Jesus, expounding his
teaching, does not after all consider that exposition to be
faithful to its original?

The ethical teaching of this Gospel is often criticized for
being too intra-mural in scope, too uninterested in duties
and ideals relating to those beyond the church and to
society at large (notably by Jack T. Sanders in *Ethics in the
New Testament*): 'love one another' is its simple, single
tenet (13.34). Thus it contrasts with the wide horizons of
duty in the other Gospels, where love of neighbour and
love of enemy are enjoined. But the ecclesial ethics of John
is part and parcel of the compact economy of his theology.
It is fully expressive of his picture of reality, where Jesus

has brought into being the defined community of those who believe in him, the visible fruit of his mission to the world. The command to love one another is less a moral injunction than one way of describing the cohesion of the church.

In one respect after another, the members of this community are enabled to share in the common properties that Father and Son have enjoyed from 'the beginning': oneness (10.30, then 17.11), activity (5.19f., then 14.12), witness (8.18, then 15.26f.), mutual indwelling (10.38. then 17.21), mission (10.36, then 17.18; 20.21), love (15.10, 12), and even being 'in the bosom' (1.18, then 13.23, 25). By means of these pairings, John constructs a doctrine of salvation by extension of relationship. The church now enjoys that which Father and Son have always enjoyed and with not the least diminution of intensity (14.12 'greater works'). Appropriately, the second term in these pairs occurs in the supper discourses, delivered within the enclosure of the room, the church's symbolic location for John; the first term having come in the first twelve chapters where Jesus sets out the secure base of his mission and challenge before the world – in his eternal relationship with the Father. Only in one notable term is Jesus' uniqueness preserved and a clear distinction drawn: he is 'Son', believers are 'children', a distinction all the more striking in that 'son(s) of God' had been readily used of both Jesus and Christians in Paul and the other Gospels, whether unreflectively or with doctrinal purpose (see Brendan Byrne, *'Sons of God'* – *'Seed of Abraham'*), but in any case creating no confusion about the special role and person of Jesus. John, however, makes this clarification and it is his novelty. It is made, significantly, in the area of christology where this author was both most sensitive and, in the doctrine of the pre-existent and incarnate Word that receives such a prominent position, most innovative. In ecclesial terms, he may have felt it prudent to sound a note of caution against a certain style of identification of Christ and believers which left no clear place for differentiation: Jesus is no less 'lord and master' of his followers for being also 'friend' (13.13f., 15.15). But the false turn is a development to which the 'in Christ' language of both Paul and John is susceptible in certain circumstances, for example where ecstasy suppresses reason.

Compared with the actual verbal pervasiveness of christology, there is a sense in which John's ecclesiology has to be inferred. Nevertheless, it seems perverse to deny that it is a presence throughout his work, an assumption in all his theology; partly because the church framework of life was simply taken for granted, and partly because of the virtual inclusion of ecclesiology within christology or, to put the matter a little more modestly, its total derivation from it and dependence on it.

This 'church' assumption is confirmed at a more practical level by the suggestions, made by J. L. Martyn, R. E. Brown (see especially the latter's *Community of the Beloved Disciple*) and others, for seeing abundant evidence in the Gospel for the history, make-up and church relations of the community in which it was written. On this view, passages that have commonly been taken as simple reminiscences of Jesus' life-time, or else, more critically, as to a large degree Johannine literary creations, testify to actualities of the community's life. Thus, the material about John the Baptist, recurring so perplexingly, is to be explained by the inclusion in this church of former adherents of the Baptist and by his status in relation to Jesus being still an unresolved question. And the seemingly innocent (perhaps in part traditional, in part fictive) references to Peter, Thomas and others of the Twelve conceal allusions to other Christian communities that are in the ken of the Johannine church, and with which it has relations in part friendly and in part critical, and to which it feels a certain superiority expressed in the unique closeness of its eponymous hero (and founder?), the beloved disciple, to Jesus (13.23; 20.8). All this would speak more for ecclesiastical rather than ecclesiological (practical rather than theoretical) awareness; though the two aspects converge in the figure of the beloved disciple in so far as he may be taken to represent Johannine 'specialness' in theological insight and not merely those Christians' existence as a distinct group within the church as a whole. The closeness to Jesus surely represents awareness of possessing perceptions and ideas of peculiar power and cohesion. At least, the Johannine church had every reason to make such an estimate of itself. It might have its limitations in modern eyes ('the Jews'? the ethic of loving 'one another'?), but its theological achievement was prodigious both in its sheer conceptual tenacity from the beginning to the end of the book and in the audacity of the Logos christology advanced in the prologue.

If ecclesiology may be seen as 'higher' when the Christian community has a strong sense of its own enclosedness from the world and from the complication of relations with other societies, then Johannine ecclesiology merits this description. It is particularly notable, by comparison with not only Paul but also Mark, Matthew and Luke, for the relative absence of complexity in the picture of the role of Judaism in God's purpose. In the Fourth Gospel, we find little sign of agonizing on this issue – no real parallel to Paul's struggle to make sense of the continuity of God's people from Abraham, through Jesus and gentile incorporation to an ultimate conclusion, alongside a conviction of Jesus as representing a new departure, even a re-start of creation itself. It is true there is a kind of sadness in John that 'he came to his own property and his own people did not receive him' (1.11), but this is speedily overtaken by the demonization of 'the Jews' (8.44), depicted as the enemies of Jesus and of God himself, the personification of the darkness that is inexorably and, it seems, irredeemably opposed to the light which is Jesus. Even more than in the other Gospels, it is the Jews rather than Pilate who are responsible for the extinguishing of the light by crucifixion – which is nevertheless the consummation of glory. It is true that some Jews side with Jesus (7.43; 10.19) and others make serious moves towards him (3.1ff.), perhaps reflecting the actual experience of the Johannine Christians in their own dealings. But it is only as they truly come to him (become his disciples, as Joseph of Arimathea and Nicodemus, 19.38–40) that they can be reckoned to have left the darkness. In 8.31, we meet Jews 'who believed in him', but for John their faith is woefully inadequate as they will not renounce their Abrahamic pride (like one side of Paul, Rom.11.1) and grasp the absoluteness of Christ's superiority to him (8.58), and so of the Christian community's supersession of the Jewish. Note that the church too, like Jesus, has a kind of pre-existence: 'from the beginning' (15.27).

It is also true that John sees the old scriptures as fulfilled in Jesus, both in terms of particular texts and in symbols like the temple (2.21; 7.38f.), the vine (15.1–17), and the shepherd and flock (10.1–18), where Jesus and the church step naturally into Israel's shoes. For John, the authors of scripture are on Jesus' side and privy to the truth about him. They know of him (5.46) and have seen him (12.41), just as Abraham is, as it were, within Jesus' grasp (8.58). John does not, alas, make the connection fully explicit, but this attitude to the scriptures makes sense if Jesus is not only pre-existent as the Word but is also identified with 'the word' as scripture (cf. Ecclus. 24.23). Perhaps this is the understanding in terms of which we are to read the only apparently pro-Jewish statement, 'salvation is of the Jews' (4.22); though in large part its sense is determined by its context, as stating an anti-Samaritan preference in the limited issue of Jew versus Samaritan. Aspects of Torah are referred to (sabbath in ch.5 and circumcision in 8.22f.) but by way of debating points not as live issues for the Johannine church itself. John 1.17 comes nearest to making the connection. In relation to Judaism and Israel, John's ecclesiology reveals a new, clear-cut quality: for him, the church is tidier at the edges, socially and histori-cally, as ch. 9 most clearly demonstrates – one is either in or out, and Christian identity is defined solely by reference to Jesus (9.38, though there is uncertainty of text in that verse).

The suggestion, made by R. A. Culpepper (*The Johannine School*), that the Johannine community should be seen, sociologically, on the model of a philosophical school of the time, may help to explain the sense of inde-pendence from other groups, though it can only be part of the story. In its scriptural 'bookishness', it was not without affinities with the ethos of the synagogue, where indeed its founding members probably had their origin, and there is every sign that it was in lively debate with Jews. Jesus' controversies that are so prominent in the first half of the Gospel (especially chs 7–8) must surely be, at the least, coloured by such present interest. Still, this church's sense of independence may have been fortified by the feeling of belonging to a different social life-style and orientation, those appropriate to a school; and the intellectual sophisti-cation of the Gospel squares well with the idea that this forms at least part of the group's identity. Such a role would help to give a feeling of social location to a group now cut off (9.22; 16.2) from its original roots, which, theologically as well as socially, it now forswore, with the support of some of its most cherished convictions, notably that Jesus was the universal Word.

Be that as it may, when we turn to the Johannine Epistles (which I take to reflect developments subsequent to the writing of the Gospel), we find certain novelties and changes in relation to ecclesiology. The eye is caught first by the fact that the word 'church' now makes an appearance (III John 6,9,10); but it carries no doctrinal resonance, as far as we can tell, though its appearance only in such a largely down-to-earth piece of writing as III John makes it impossible to be sure that in other contexts it might not have had doctrinal significance.

Much more interesting is the ominous (and pregnant) shift in the relation of ecclesiology to christology. Formerly, as we saw, the Johannine Christians regarded the two as closely integrated with each other: the church is simply the adherents of Jesus, those in whom he dwells and who dwell in him. Now, however, the church is defined (by the writer of I John) not as the community of those who believe in Jesus but as the community of those who hold correct beliefs about him. There is no need here to identify the content of the right and the wrong beliefs as the writer would define them (see the commentaries, e.g. those of R. E. Brown or the present writer). The significant point is that ecclesiology is here no longer defined simply by belief in Jesus, with the church as the society of those who come to him, but by a particular form of that belief, with the church as those who not only come to him but do it with certain beliefs clear in their minds and other beliefs deliberately discarded. Among the Christians themselves, and the Johannine Christians at that, there are the accepted and the rejected. It could of course have been otherwise. Ecclesiology might, as it were, have stood its ground. The church, as the people of Jesus, might have stood by its need to include all who attached themselves to him. In the Johannine case, it chose to be the servant of christological correctness. In so doing, it made an ominous decision as far as the future of the church was concerned. At the very least, the former smooth harmony, even virtual fusion, between christology and ecclesiology, so sublimely epitomized in John 17, was disrupted. This move is of course ominous also in that the writer of I John is so wholly convinced of his party's monopoly of rightness and of being the true community of Jesus' adherents that his sense of outrage at the falsehood of his opponents precludes reconciliation and moderation, whether on ecclesiological or ethical grounds: 'love' itself, now defined as the nature of God himself (4.8), is narrowed to the 'true' brothers, those with whom the author agrees. Yet all this is combined with the most sublime Johannine language about God's unique gift of Jesus as the bringer of salvation (4.1–21). It was a situation whose pattern was to be reproduced countless times in the church's history.

Earlier, I drew a sharp contrast between the itinerant, rural and non-institutional character of Jesus' ministry and the urban, settled character of the Pauline (and subsequent) communities. Though that is surely both correct and significant for our subject, lying at the root of lasting tensions, we can now refine the picture; for it is as if a sense or even portrait of the later church and its life is superimposed (like a patterned transparent sheet) in the Gospels upon the basic presentation within which Jesus comes before our eyes.

4

Other Strands and Tendencies

The purpose of this book so far has not been to give an exhaustive account of material relating to the church even in the range of writings discussed. Rather it has been to draw out the logic of the leading strands in Paul and the evangelists that bear on this aspect of early Christian awareness. Two subjects stand out in high relief: first, the need to make sense in some way of the standing of the new movement stemming from Jesus in relation to Judaism, in relation to which it was both offspring and alien; and second, the conviction that, however the person of Jesus was thought of, belief about the Christian community must depend on that and be secondary to it. In other words, the church had no reason to exist that was not wholly bound up with him, whether in the light of the memory of his earthly career, his present lordship or his future open triumph.

We shall not attempt to deal in detail with the rest of the New Testament writings, but there are certain other strands, mostly discernible in the later books, which need our attention. They carry matters beyond the two topics just summarized, partly by way of diversion into unsurprising new channels, partly entering on paths that were to be more determinative, in many different ways, for the future history of the church.

In the first place, there was a growing capacity to have

in view the church as a whole, rather than as the local congregation or as a collection of such congregations. As we saw, Paul already inaugurates this sense in some of his uses of 'church', as does Matthew in 16.17. It is less surprising in the case of Paul that this development should occur, given his wide-ranging relationship to numerous Christian groups over a vast territory. It is not clear how this shift in usage (if that is how we should see it) took place, but it is securely established in Colossians and in (the probably post-Pauline and pseudonymous) Ephesians (Col. 1.18, 24; Eph. 1.22; 3.10, 21; 5.23–32). It is left to Ignatius of Antioch in the early second century to formalize the concept by explicitly distinguishing the local from the 'universal' church (*catholike ekklesia*), though the latter is authentically discernible in the former, Christ being encountered in the one as truly as in the other (Ign. Smyrneans 8.2).

Secondly, there is a tendency in some of the later New Testament writings frankly to 'de-theologize' the church; that is to begin to discuss it simply as an institution within society, needing to take care of relations with those around. In such cases, it is much too grand to speak of 'beliefs about' the church, for the religious context seems to have slipped out of sight as far as this subject is concerned. In social terms, we may see this as the church having come of age. It is setting off on the long road of secular involvements, littered with a limitless sequence of complex situations and insoluble problems. We feel this in the Pastoral Epistles, especially in I Tim. 2.1–4, where the aspiration is for 'a quiet and peaceable life, godly and respectful in every way'. Nowhere in these three documents do we find reflection on the place of the Christian community in Christian belief. More attention focusses on the officers or leaders of the community, not exactly on their place in a structure of belief but rather on their proper qualifications (I Tim. 3). We do learn, however, that the household remains the favoured model for the church (v.5).

Thirdly, there is the beginning of a tendency, briefly adumbrated by Paul in Phil. 3.20, to view the church in the light of the infinitely greater heavenly community of the court of God, both as present context for the earthly church and as its future destiny. This too had a rich future ahead of it, both theologically and, notably, in the understanding and words of the eucharistic liturgy, seen as celebrated in union with 'all the company of heaven'. The fact that this and the preceding tendency vie with one another in theory and in psychology has not prevented their co-existing in the minds and conduct of many Christians, especially those responsible for the direction of the public affairs of the church. The one may be seen as compensation for or rebound from the other, or, better, as the legitimate correcting of vision.

In a way, the contrast appears already in the Revelation of John, which attends first to the all-too-earthly life of seven churches of the province of Asia (chs 2–3), and then to the heavenly court, the true backcloth to their present life and the scene in which their future destiny is to be revealed and played out. A sense of the church's destiny also pre-occupies the Letter to the Hebrews, where again there is no theology (to speak of) about the present church, but where there is a grand assurance of the 'heavenly Jerusalem', to which earthly Christians can be said already to 'have come' . The heavenly community is called 'the church of the first-born enrolled in heaven'. It is the culmination of the thoroughgoing process whereby Jesus and the dispensation inaugurated by him have subsumed and superseded all the arrangements for salvation laid down in the Torah liturgies. Ephesians too has a heavenly perspective, differently, Paulinely expressed, but having the same thrust and direction.

We should note that one element in the Christian experience of the church that was to be paramount in later centuries makes no appearance in the New Testament; that is, the church as the carrier and guardian of folk-religion, hallowing the great cyclical events of the year, of nature, and of human life, including rites of passage for the individual and the family. We simply have no idea what the New Testament Christians did to mark birth, marriage or death, even though we have some knowledge of their reactions to the last (e.g. in I Thess. 4 and I Cor. 15). That mode of the church's existence, which still colours its whole being even where it exists in post-Christian social settings, makes virtually no appearance in what we know of the churches of the first century. Its absence (if absent it really was) differentiated them significantly from both Judaism and the prevailing paganism. For a while in its common life, and for ever through the continuing use of these early writings, we may say that the church thereby had the chance to re-define the very meaning of religion itself. No wonder there has been sometimes a reluctance in parts of the churches to accept wholeheartedly the responsibilities of being the handlers of folk-religion.

5

Is There a Message?

The attempt to consider the New Testament material on
any subject, with minimal pre-conceptions from the later
history of Christianity, is likely to provoke a dual response
in the modern Christian: a sense partly of alienation,
partly of recognition. There may even be a disturbing
suspicion that if the recognition outweighs the alienation
to a greater degree than in the case, for example, of a work
of popular mediaeval piety or a Saxon manual of Christian
healing rituals, this is only because of the long tradition of
domestication in the case of the New Testament which has
acclimatized it to each successive age. Nevertheless, one is
sometimes likely to come away from the New Testament
feeling one has encountered people, many of whose preoccupations and assumptions seem so remote from ours
that it takes an effort of both education and sympathy to
enter into them, aided no doubt by an imaginative feel for
partial parallels in modern circumstances. At the same
time, the New Testament people are recognizably sharers
with us in allegiance and devotion, and indeed in the
essence of some of the problems confronting them, whatever the difference between their ancient and modern
forms. Moreover, their terminology and ideas (however
doused in modernity) are constantly before us in talk and
worship. The application of present-day gloss, whether
deliberately in updating work on liturgy and Bible or

unconsciously through the accommodations of our minds, does not modernize as much as may be intended, though it may do something to suppress the properly alienating elements. Deciding which of the two judgments and reactions is more appropriate in any particular case is not easy; anyway, the establishing of our response is often done at a level below that of conscious decision. This may happen not only in informal situations but also in the use of the New Testament in the process of the construction of mature theological or ethical judgments.

Sticking to the New Testament's own content, let us (at some risk of tedium, but the topic refuses to go away) consider the dominant issue in the self-understanding of the first generation of Christians: their relation to Judaism (or, to put it less anachronistically, to other manifestations of Judaism than their own). Though it was not as important a factor in their self-understanding as a community as their allegiance to Jesus, this was undoubtedly the dominant *issue*. It arose partly for external reasons (there were Jews who raised it) and partly for internal reasons (it was necessary for them to define both Jesus and themselves in some way by reference to the God-given scriptures of their inheritance). Of course this issue was interwoven with their allegiance to Jesus: how else, apart from pure subjective judgment, looking like mere arbitrary enthusiasm (its inexplicability was what worried Paul about ecstatic glossolalia, I Cor. 14), could that allegiance receive backing? The only accepted basis for debate with (other) Jews and for giving intellectual satisfaction to themselves was the interpretation of scripture. It had to be shown that the claims made by Jesus and on his behalf were scripturally grounded – and indeed that they represented the correct interpretation of scripture.

Not many modern Christians would place this concern

at the heart of their allegiance to Jesus. With the New
Testament so long established among us, appeal is much
more likely to be made to its witness to him, whether his
story or his teaching, or indeed to teaching about him by
Paul and others, rather than to prophetic or other texts in
the Old Testament; and if the appeal is not to the New
Testament, then it will be to the Jesus of the church, the
Jesus of formal dogma, or the Jesus of the multi-faceted
experience of Christians down the centuries. The church's
independence and validity in this respect seems self-
evident, and there is ordinarily no need to argue for its
right in principle to make claims for Jesus or to give him a
central role, though one might disagree with the form of
those claims and the description of that role.

Similarly, the question of the church's relation to
Judaism from which, as a matter of history, it derived, in
the beginning and at least in part, is no longer one that
usually occasions Christian anxiety. It is not normally the
case that, unless this question can be satisfactorily
answered, the church has no sense of its validity in the
world, no way of making sense of itself. Mostly, it pro-
ceeds without giving the matter a thought. In this perspective, Paul's feeling for the essentially free-standing newness
of Christ, a new Adam at the head of a new creation, won
the day over his anguished and ingenious determination to
show how the scriptures properly and inevitably led up to
Jesus, from whom, as Messiah, their ultimate fulfilment
would derive. This victory was no doubt partly a matter of
the lapse of time and of a consequent shift in perspective.
The church, increasingly dominant in society, was here to
stay and physically in Europe Judaism was marginal if
rarely quite uncontroversial. So the church stood in little
need of fundamental argument for its self-sufficient
existence; though there was of course a lasting place for

apologetic aimed at a variety of audiences, Jews among them. Not that the Pauline arguments for the fulfilment of an age-long scriptural process were denied or abandoned; rather, for the most part, they lost their urgency and their capacity to produce anguish in Christian hearts. On the fringes of the church, they might of course, from time to time, be taken to authorize proselytizing activities towards Jews as a distinct group. The broader question of the church's relation to Judaism did not however wholly disappear from the scene, even though it fell into the background for whole tracts of time and space, and from time to time it has assumed prominence, usually with disastrous results for the Jewish minority facing dominant Christian authorities. Where there has been debate, it has usually taken forms derived in some form from scripture, often monotonously so. But the very disparity in terms of power of the two parties where they have collided in the course of Christian history has given the debate a wholly different context from that of early Christianity, when the arguments were first formulated. Then, the church was struggling against heavy odds to establish a hearing and to find a scripturally reasonable basis for identity; while Judaism, diverse as it was, had assured ways of understanding itself in the face of which the church's claims often seemed perverse or eccentric and the interpretation given to key texts contrived. The debate was for the church of that time a matter of sheer necessity, of intellectually defensible survival; later it became rather an academic luxury, sometimes verging on the trivial, or else an instrument of oppression.

With certain noble exceptions over the centuries, it is only in recent years, with the growth in some Western countries of inter-faith dialogue, that the picture has shown signs of changing; and even in these new conditions, it has not proved easy to transcend the traditional terms of debate and controversy. Neither Jews nor Christians find it easy to see their faith in other than the most traditional terms or to abandon the sterile postures of long ago. There is a tendency in both camps to dwell on the period of Christian origins, as if, within this capsule of beliefs and thought-patterns, nothing had changed.

Yet the truth is that even an elementary historical understanding of the Bible and its times renders the old debates otiose and obsolete. Their terms were set in circumstances so different from our own; and both Judaism and Christianity have developed down the years along such different and complex paths that the debates and battles found in the New Testament (themselves diverse to the point of inconsistency) no longer have intelligible force. Modern debates between Judaism and Christianity have to take cognizance of the world-setting (including other world-faiths and our own internal complexities) in which we both live. Both sides, in so far as they are able to reach objectivity about themselves, can recognize internal developments that place the old controversies (e.g. over the role of Christ) in a new and softer light. A sympathetic historical understanding of the situations reflected in the New Testament is surely an indispensable aid to the process of adjustment.

There is one New Testament metaphor for the Christian community that, if developed in certain ways, may offer hope of convergence. Historical surveys such as that in Heb. 11 and the application to the church of some of the attributes of Israel, as in I Peter 2.9 and Rev. 1.6 (echoing Ex. 19.6) offer a sense of communal continuity less complex and tortuous than that in Rom. 9–11, though, from a Jewish point of view, equally imperialistic – for the church is the culmination of the process ordained by God

('apart from us they should not be made perfect',
Heb. 11.40). Nevertheless, it is a metaphor of both com-
munality and mobility through history. Taken not as a
doctrine but as a suggestive image, it offers a sense of
openness to developments as yet undreamt of. Who can
tell in what form the people of God will in future manifest
itself and which types of individuals and groupings may
not find a place in this procession? Most obviously lending
itself to positive intra-Christian ecumenical ends, this
imagery (powerfully fostered at Vatican II) also has
possibilities for inter-faith relations, even those between
Christianity and Judaism, to which at first sight it seems so
inimical. As we have seen, however, models of continuity,
though present already in Paul and perhaps serviceable in
this way for some modern causes, are not the dominant
expression of Christian self-understanding: the theoretical
and dogmatic centrality of Christ as all-sufficient and as
God's novum has generally combined with institutional
preoccupations to foster the church's self-sufficiency and
exclusivity. This is not the place to consider how far a
historical understanding of Jesus, such as this book has
applied to the church of New Testament times, can
suitably bring any mitigation of that exclusivity, putting
the matter into a different key from that of the doctrinal
tradition, which itself owes its impulse to the stronger
assertions about Jesus to be found in the New Testament
and was formed at a time when there was every reason to
make clear lines of division from Jewish styles of thought
and indeed from the forces which had brought about
Jesus' death.

Another tension in earliest Christianity has bequeathed
to us an equally problematic legacy for our understanding
of the church. In a sense it is a matter of structure rather
than belief, yet the two cannot be wholly separated. We

saw that the picture of Jesus' activity in the gospels is of a rural movement (there is no reference to the major towns of Northern Palestine) that resisted the formation of permanent groups and was content with brief encounters with individuals and crowds. The only continuity resided in the itinerant group of Jesus and the Twelve. In so far as we 'read' this picture in ecclesial terms, we are likely to focus on that group; yet in many ways it is ill-suited to that purpose – all male, mobile, virtually unstructured, without any of the apparatus of social stability. As far as the Gospels are concerned, both these objects or fruits of Jesus' ministry (the short-term individuals and crowds and the long-term Twelve) make problematic models for the seeker after guidance about the church. The former must apparently repent and absorb Jesus' teaching or enjoy the God-given release (e.g. from blindness or madness) which Jesus has mediated to them; the latter must learn and follow, then be missioners on Jesus' behalf and on the model of his own work. In any case, the Twelve contrast with the groups encountered in Paul's letters: urban, organized, settled, long-term. Here, the term *ekklesia* is applied with complete suitability. Here, from the modern point of view, 'the church' begins to be recognizable. Yet the situation in Jesus' ministry shares, and often dominates, our field of vision: and the church of subsequent times never knows where to focus its gaze. Two distinct pictures of Christian life retain authority: in practice, the Pauline urban church predominates, even, in due course, in the countryside; and Christian missions follow the pattern not of Jesus (except initially) but of Paul, establishing workable Christian communities everywhere. But the vision of Jesus' mode of action remains, as impossible but not discardable ideal and as irritant: should we too not have a similar freedom from the ties of structures, social and domestic, that bedevil our capacity to be communities that are recognizable as followers (as distinct from worshippers or servants) of Jesus? It was the urbanization of Christianity, no doubt ante-dating Paul (Jerusalem, Antioch) but nevertheless supremely his achievement, that chiefly brought 'church' into being as the characteristic mode of Christian existence – so much so that even the great majority of those seeking to live in renewed obedience to Jesus' life-style, abandoning goods and family, have done it in communities, with the solitary or itinerant style of the religious life always a minority taste. Other factors, like the fading of a realistic apocalyptic hope, contributed of course to the elaboration of ecclesial structures, but it was urbanization that led to their establishment – and so to what remains for ever, surely, a source of discomfort in the Christian conscience that is inherent in our origins and in the dual witness of the New Testament documents. It must be admitted that this discomfort is overwhelmingly tolerated without, it seems, too much difficulty; but it keeps asserting itself, and those outside the church often find the occasion of it more natural than those inside. Should such assertion be encouraged? It does not easily sit as one item on a long agenda.

Christian social witness, with its concentration on the needy in their various manifestations, owes its inspiration not to the earliest churches as we see them in Paul's letters, but to the model of the Gospels. If we look on those churches as experimental and embryonic examples of Christian common life, then we have to admit that they offer little incentive to Christians to follow major aspects of the mission of Jesus himself. Their sense of obligation to those who lacked was, it seems, generally limited to their own members (Acts 4.32ff., Rom. 12.13, together with the rather grudging provision for widows – for how many in the first century survived until they were sixty? – in I Tim.5); on the other side, there is only the generality of Rom. 12.8 and 13.9, where the real objects of generosity in mind are left unspecified. In other words, the social vision of the Christian witness has been kept alive essentially by literary means (the reading of the Gospels, e.g. Matt. 25.31–46; Luke 4.18ff., 10.25–37, 16.19–31) rather than structural, ecclesial means. To a degree indeed the two visions or concerns have been in tension, or separated, in Christian life. To this day, it is not unknown for Christians engaged in Christ-like generosity to cause unease to church authorities which at the least may interpose a measure of institutional formality (e.g. by way of theological or procedural vetting) to temper the spontaneity of individuals. Not unknown for the internal needs of the institution of the church to battle it out with the unbounded claims of the poor and needy. At the same time, the ideal of the Christian community as a place of generous love has from earliest times been not only a beacon to others but also among the inspirations of charitable activity, and indeed Christian communities (themselves sometimes on the margins of church life) have often been its agents.

Transcending this practical tension is the simple fact that, however diversely it is expressed, christology is the driving force of most New Testament understandings of the Christian community. It is a body of people whose reason for being relates solely to Christ. This concentration is fundamentally simple as a religion's basis compared with, for example, a book of laws for life and cult or a collection of normative myths; but it makes many manifestations of the church down the ages seem diffuse and disordered, or else over-burdened with required tenets and duties. Often ecclesiology has been less a function of christology than an independent body of teaching and debate, with external links to political authorities and, internally, a concentration on the proprieties of the conditions for the church's ministers. It is arguable that the tendency to give the church a kind of theological autonomy in this way, even to make it determinative for supposedly more basic doctrines (as when sharing in communion is denied to fellow-Christians of – contradiction in terms! – another communion than one's own), begins to show itself already in some of the New Testament writings. In the Pauline tradition, for example, the strong integration of Christ and church in I Corinthians, so striking in its intensity, is relaxed in Ephesians and Colossians, where Christ as head is, for all his connectedness to the church, nevertheless distinguishable from it. This distinctness, masked in Ephesians by the high-flown character of the language but nonetheless real, betokens a shift in consciousness which has prevailed in church life over the great majority of times and places; except in the intensity of prayer and worship, where the vision may be regained. The same contrast can be drawn between Luke-Acts and the Gospel of John: while the latter breathes an air of the most intense union of Christ with his own, the former sees him as removed to heaven exercising lordship from a distance, even over those who serve him in the power of the Spirit.

It can be said of course that this distancing of the church from Christ is the merest realism, and a salutary guard against foolish self-idolizing by the church, to which in any case it has often been all too prone, and more in the pursuit of power than the expression of devotion. All the same, it represents a move by the church to find other sources of significance and reason for existing. It is a move towards less spiritually strenuous styles of identity.

The disparity between the christologically determined integration and the more independent sense of the church's being is of course a persisting feature of church life. The former has a tendency to be placed in the sphere of spirituality – it is felt interiorly and expressed in gatherings for prayer; the latter is generally the determinant of church policy-making and daily activity. Is that inevitable or might more robust thought find ways of allowing ideas of Christ to colour more thoroughly the priorities and decisions of churches? Might there at least be more obvious signs that a struggle towards this end had taken place?

The contrast just described is often expressed in sociological terms and focussed on the development of the church's structure of leaders. It represents an ineluctable development from an initial phase (in Jesus' activity and, in different mode, in Paul's first churches), where the old is turned upside down and the world is made new, to a stage of routinization where institutions, needed for sheer survival and stability, acquire their own life and their own justification (see, for example, Peter L. Berger and Thomas Luckman, *The Social Construction of Reality*, and Berger, *The Social Reality of Religion*). Of course there are theories to build the institutions into the inherited faith, but these are a comfort to mind and soul rather than the motive force of the institutions' emergence. Cut the flannel, a realist might say, an incipient clergy soon comes to exist in practice for its own sake, with its own rules and customs, in one respect after another on all fours with comparable elements of other human organizations. And the same may be said of the church's central rites like baptism and eucharist. Does not every organization need means whereby to initiate and then to hold and encourage its members in their allegiance – never mind the impulse which gave rise to it all in the first place?

The depressing tone of such an account is misplaced and other reactions are entirely possible and more realistic. A first step indeed is to accept the analysis and indeed to intensify its apparent power to dismay. For it seems that while institutional features undoubtedly became more formal and significant in the last part of the New Testament period (and then permanently), they were far from absent even in the first Pauline communities. And common sense suggests that, though it does not show through reliably in the Gospel record, Jesus' own movement cannot have been free of organizational arrangements. In I Corinthians, for example, Paul is at pains to replace the socially more powerful Christians by his own nominees (I Cor. 16.15–17), on whom he will rely for a structure of administration that will allow more scope to a wider range of Christian gifts. It is christologically motivated organization, but organization none the less. And how could it have been otherwise in any human community whatsoever? There is neither sign nor possibility that Christianity can or could ever have been a 'spiritual' faith without an institutional dimension, however regrettable it is that the institutional element has often, from early days, tended to obscure the fundamental thrust of the gospel message and to generate a life of its own. From our point of view, therefore, as was suggested above, it is not so much that an original holy anarchy is replaced by hierarchical institutions as that the latter element begins to develop its own rationale, both within a Christian framework (e.g. ideas of succession from apostles as necessary to validity in the mainstream church, as developed from the second century) and in a spirit of ordinary social decency and good sense (e.g. the job description for leaders in I Tim. 3). Of course there is a certain necessity and inevitability here, as the founder's charismatic, world-shifting impulse (itself prone

to exaggeration and misconception – for it too had a pre-history and a context) becomes a matter of custom and inheritance, and as new social contexts and the changing social composition of the church itself (more gentiles, more second and third-generation Christians) alter the character of the church's life. But whatever the pressures for change in these ways, the stronger, christological vision of the church did not disappear, even if practicalities were an obstacle to its effectiveness or rather posed new challenges for its implementation; for the documents that enshrined that vision continued to be circulated, read and indeed, in the course of the second century, acquired greater, canonical force. To survive is of necessity to change and to adapt.

The New Testament ideas of the church differed from ours in their basic, often unspoken sense of the church's transience, at least in its existing form. Transience was inherent in any theory or idea one might then have of the church. We saw this expressed most vividly in the Revelation of John, both in its proportions and in its content; but it colours the whole New Testament. Yet it is not that 'Christian community' will not survive into the new age. Quite the contrary, however it is constituted (and both Paul and the Revelation have ideas about that), the community will be at the centre of the scene. But leaving that future aside, we attend to the effect of this perspective on the church's sense of itself in the present. Here is yet another tension in early Chrsitianity itself and bequeathed to later times down to the present. There is plenty of room for formal contradiction. If the church, as presently embodied, is transient, how much effort is it worth investing, not only in the elaboration of leadership structures, but also in detailed rules for the complexity of human conduct, in principles to govern relations with political authorities, in the precise definition of theological beliefs, in the finding and safeguarding of financial provision, and, in due course, in buildings and their embellishment, subject to fire, pillage and ruination? Of course, all this has subsequently grown to mammoth proportions, and eschatological hope has come to assume in part an air of make-believe or to be confined to an annual spurt of attention in Advent; or else to be the subject of occasional panic, or to be individualized as one contemplates one's own mortality. There have indeed been times when it has dominated Christian consciousness and Christian groups for whom it remains the constant preoccupation; but even then it does not always obliterate concern for building repairs, insurance policies and pension schemes. We happen now to be in a time when for many Western Christians, in their prosperity, the eschatological hope is peculiarly dim or else almost wholly interiorized and individualized: 'the church', where attended to at all, is for other things, chiefly moral and educational, and for friendship and the fulfilment of spiritual needs.

This tension, or distinction at least, is not invisible even in the church of the New Testament. The Gospel of Matthew, for example, combines the careful provision of rules for church life (ch.18) with a vivid sense of apocalypse (chs 24–25) – to which indeed obedience to moral rules is directly related. In II Thessalonians there is a concern to maintain the duties of the present age, even in the context of fervent hope (ch.3). Yet elsewhere the tension is slackened, in one direction or the other. In the constituting of what has been called the guild of widows (I Tim. 5), we surely see provision only for this age – unless the heavenly categorizing of Christians according to status in the church, found in the art of later times, was already creeping into Christian imagination. In the Gospel of John, by contrast, the almost total neglect of helpful ethics betokens a sense that Christians are in effect living already in the new age, here and now. Could the Johannine church have organized practical relief? Perhaps it could, to judge from I John 3.17.

The loss of a sense of tension in this area is serious for a viable Christian idea of the church. Only the retaining of that sense can justify the church's claims and missionary aims, and without it, those claims become pretensions. True, it is possible to avoid this predicament. For example, in the high Middle Ages, the Western church was so powerful, so essential to the working of government at every level, that one could be overwhelmed by its strength as a presence in the world. It is not surprising that some of the challenges to that power came from Christians who sought to redress the balance under the impulse of the New Testament, by appealing both to the simplicity of gospel life and to a revived apocalyptic sense. Or else by contrast we may think of Christian communities, past and present, which succeed in isolating themselves from the surrounding society, feeling no responsibility for its ills and woes, being as it were angelic enclaves, anticipations of the new age. At least such bodies preserve a live sense of 'the other' and of the future which is virtually absent from many of the larger Christian bodies. If any proper sense is to be made of love for the church, and if such love is to avoid over-attachment to the institution and the ignoring of its faults, there must be some element of 'otherness', some sense that the church is essentially a community transcending the present age. Here indeed christology and eschatology meet as, however expressed, dimensions of Christian awareness that dominate the idea of the church. There are of course numerous ways in which these dimensions have been formulated, not always in very close integration with an idea of the church – with which, in the New Testament, they are so integrally bound.

With regard to some modern preoccupations in relation to the church, notably ecumenism and questions of the 'validity' of particular Christian bodies, the New Testament, viewed in a realistic historical light, has little useful to say. The questions had not arisen. True, there are in that early period examples for us to ponder, but their usefulness to us is limited – the circumstances were so different from ours. For instance, the paradigm of schism in I John both horrifies and stimulates thought about its justification: was it too lightly done? what kind of issue would justify schism? Generally, in past and present, Christians have been inclined to tread that path for reasons much less fundamental than those adduced in I John. Can that be right, on any reasonable New Testament idea of the church? Paul's break with Peter because Peter had broken fellowship with gentile converts (Gal. 2.11ff.) is more tragic and baffling still: for here the break comes in the name of the greater vision of unity itself. Or, in other terms, the centre of existing validity is forsaken in order that the only possible future Christian validity may emerge and be established; that is, in a community open on equal terms to all humans in allegiance to Christ alone. The (surely idealized and fictional?) agreement in Acts 15, so devoid of visible historical effect, seems to point to the futility of compromise – a barren price for a poor kind of unity. It has a symbolic grandeur in the sweep of Luke's tale of the spread of the gospel, but outside that context it has no role.

These examples from the New Testament period (and they could be extended in sharper terms, see Michael Goulder, *A Tale of Two Missions*) discourage any romantic idea that the church once was one, only to be rent in later times by heretics and wilful schismatics – the classical theory of the matter. The Fathers traced such wickedness to the second-century gnostics; it is apparent that it goes back to the church's very roots.

Does this then consign ecumenism, in its fuller sense of the quest for the visible organic unity of all Christians, to a limbo of dreams? And does it indicate the arbitrary character of the confident claims still made about criteria for validity among Christian bodies? (Not, to be clear, because the New Testament can sensibly dictate our policies, but because it can suggest lines of reflection and proportions of value that we do well to consider.)

With regard to ecumenism, it seems that in a New Testament perspective there is no question of recapturing an original unfractured oneness of the Christian community. In any significant and identifiable sense, there never was any such thing. What is more, though there is plenty of antagonism to those seen as deviants by those whose views we read (opponents' views rarely come to us in their own words and, unless the Letter of James is in part directed at the teaching of Paul, we hear no advocates for them), as in I John and Galatians, it does not quite take the form of attacking them for breaking up a pristine unity of the church. Modern ecumenism in practice has sought to repair some selected much more recent breaks, like those between Rome and Byzantium and of the sixteenth-century Reform, and 'the scandal of disunity' refers in practice chiefly to those ecclesiastical breaks that are part of Europe's historical consciouness. It might be said that attention to these ruptures, often in terms of their origin which lies deep in the past and bears little relation to present-day concerns, has diverted attention from reflection on the fundamentals of Christian unity-and-division which the New Testament might suggest to us.

But is there not in John 17 a dominical injunction
to unity – 'that they all may be one' – that has both
authorized and enforced the modern quest for church
unity? Again it has to be said that, however inspiring those
words have proved to modern Christians and whatever
merits the ecumenical cause may or may not have, in a
New Testament historical perspective, their original use
had no eye on the aspirations of twentieth-century
Christians. It is open to discussion indeed whether they
had a pragmatic reference (for example, to some aspect of
the church situation in the evangelist's context) or, as most
interpreters have thought, this speech by Jesus is of such
sublimity that its author's mind was far removed from the
everyday circumstances of the Christian community but
concerned rather with the profound unity of all Christians,
perhaps of the human race, in him through whom all
things were made and who was the light lightening all who
come into the world. Readers who enter into the
Johannine vision may then, in more practical mode, discuss whether its purpose would best be furthered by
particular styles of ecumenical endeavour or by quite other
means of promoting human unity across quite other, and
more dangerous, human divides. The Johannine vision is,
after all, human and salvific before it is ecclesiastical, or
better, it is ecclesiastical only in being human. None of this
in itself either disparages or encourages the ecumenism of
the twentieth century. It simply leaves it to make its case
on other, perhaps less portentous grounds. It suggests,
however, that the insistence on organic unity, so difficult
to achieve and so uncertain of beneficial fruits, was always
misconceived, never worth the immense energy that
churches have felt it beholden upon them to invest in it;
and that the simple duty to love and to work with one's
fellow-Christians for all good ends should have been